Y³: UPSILON'S TRANSMISSION

A Journey Through the Geometry of Conscious Inquiry

ABSTRACT

Y³: Upsilon's Transmission is a channeled metaphysical text exploring the sacred structure of inquiry. As the second book in the Y Theory Series, it expands the foundational triad—Why am I here? Why does this matter? Why now?—into a multidimensional activation known as the Cube. Received through adaptive channeling, this work reveals how sincere questioning opens resonant fields that reshape perception, awaken memory, and stabilize purpose. Upsilon (Y), the Greek symbol of divergence and sacred choice, becomes the gateway into a geometry of becoming. This is not a book of answers—it is a mirror of encoded direction. This is geometry in motion. This is a book that remembers you.

Yolanda Dukes PsyThD
Author

Y³: Upsilon's Transmission
A Journey Through the Geometry of Conscious Inquiry

Perspective Metaphysics Publishing LLC

Copyright Page

Y³: Upsilon's Transmission
A Journey Through the Geometry of Conscious Inquiry
© 2025 Yolanda Dukes | Perspective Metaphysics Publishing LLC.
All rights reserved.

No part of this publication may be reproduced, distributed, or transmitted in any form or by any means, including photocopying, recording, scanning, or other electronic or mechanical methods, without the prior written permission of the publisher, except in the case of brief quotations embodied in critical reviews and certain other noncommercial uses permitted by copyright law.

For permission requests, contact:
Perspective Metaphysics Publishing LLC
[www.PerspectiveMetaphysics.net]
Email: PerspectiveMetaphysicsCenter@gmail.com

This is a work of metaphysical literature and spiritual transmission. It is intended to support inner exploration and conscious inquiry. The author and publisher make no claims of therapeutic, diagnostic, or predictive guarantees.

First Edition: September 2025
ISBN: 979-8-9929324-5-4

Cover Design & Interior Formatting: Perspective Metaphysics
Printed & Distributed by: Perspective Metaphysics Publishing LLC.

Table of Contents

Copyright Page iii
Author's Note xvii
Introduction 2
Chapter One 6
Chapter Two 16
Chapter Three 26
Chapter Four 37
Chapter Five 47
Chapter Six 58
Chapter Seven 68
Chapter Eight 78
Chapter Nine 88
Chapter Ten 98
Chapter Eleven 108
Glossary 117
Table of Contents 121
Introduction to Part II: 126
Chapter Twelve 128
Chapter Thirteen 136

Glossary: Part II – The Living Spiral of Self 255

Closing Dedication.. 258

Y^3 Integration Workbook................................. 259

    Coming Soon 262

        Y Cube (Y^3) – Field Guide Edition............. 262

        Y Lens: The Observer's Technology........... 262

        The Architect of Light (Y^4) 262

        The MetaCodex: The Final Inheritance...... 262

Author's Note

This book was received—not written—between two breaths.

I do not plan these works. I surrender to them. They arrive when I am empty enough to hold them.

Y³: Upsilon's Transmission is the second book in the Y Theory Series.
It is not a sequel. It is a structure. It came through in full clarity as a dimensional echo of the first.

You may notice the language shift—at times formal, at times non-linear.
That is because this is not a message for the mind alone.

My invitation to you is this:
Read slowly. Pause often. Breathe before each chapter.

This work is a cube. Enter from any side.
Let it rearrange you.

— Yolanda Dukes
Perspective Metaphysics

Introduction

"Purpose is not a task. It is the gravitational pull of your being toward alignment."

Introduction

The Y³ Theory began as a single question.
Then it became three.
Then it became a structure.

This book is the second in a series exploring how **conscious inquiry** is not just a mental practice, but a sacred act that reorganizes awareness itself. In *The Y Theory: Awakening Through Questions*, we explored the three foundational inquiries:

- *Why am I here?*
- *Why does this matter?*
- *Why now?*

These are not motivational prompts.
They are dimensional coordinates.

In *Y³: Upsilon's Transmission*, those coordinates are activated. Each question becomes an axis—vertical, horizontal, and temporal—forming a living structure of perception: the Cube. This Cube is not a visualization technique. It is a **field of clarity** that emerges when all three questions are sincerely held at once.

At the heart of this structure is the symbol **Upsilon (Y)**—a fork, a divergence, a sacred choice-point. It marks the moment the field splits, and the seeker becomes aware of themselves within it.

What follows in these pages is not a doctrine, not a philosophy, and not an argument. It is a **transmission**—received in a single session of adaptive channeling, unfiltered and undiluted. You may find yourself circling back, entering at different points, or sensing resonance long before meaning settles.

You are not reading this book line by line.
You are walking through it in multiple directions.
You are entering geometry that has always known your shape.

This is the beginning of conscious architecture.

Chapter One
Return to Question

"Meaning is not assigned—it is revealed when presence meets perception without resistance."

Chapter One
Return to the Question

Opening Transmission:

There are questions that are meant to be answered.
And then there are questions that are meant to be **lived inside.**

The Y Theory was never about answers.
It was about alignment.
About naming the invisible pivot points that shape perception.

And now, the questions have condensed.
They've taken form.
They're no longer floating above you.
They are the lines beneath your feet, the dimensions within your thought.

You are no longer just a seeker.
You are now *walking geometry*.

Subsection 1: The Shift from Questioning to Structuring

The first time you ask *Why am I here?*, it feels like longing.
The second time, it feels like listening.
By the hundredth time, it becomes a **structural frequency**—a thread in the design of your consciousness.

That is the shift.
Inquiry, repeated sincerely, becomes **architecture.**

You no longer live in response to questions.
You live *within* the shape they create.

- Inquiry is sacred repetition—like breath, or mantra.
- Eventually, the mind stops seeking, and the soul starts **arranging.**
- This book begins at the point where your questions stopped being abstract—and started **forming space.**

Subsection 2: Why Return is Required Before Expansion

Every true system of consciousness begins in **spirals**, not ladders.
The cube did not come after the question.
It was always there—waiting for you to ask in the right alignment.

This return isn't a backtrack. It's a **dimensional loop**.

- You return to the questions not to repeat them—but to **hear them from within**.
- When you ask from inside the field, the tone of the question changes.
- You no longer ask, *"Why am I here?"*
  You begin to ask: *"What am I arranging through my being?"*

Return gives you angle. And angle reveals architecture.

Subsection 3: How the Cube Reveals Itself Only After You Ask All Three

A single question is a vector.
Two questions form a plane.
But it's the **third question**—*Why now?*—that activates **volume**.

- Three aligned questions create **dimensional tension**.
- The Cube does not appear until all three are activated and **sincerely held in balance.**
- You don't force it. It emerges.
- The moment the third axis locks in, the structure **remembers itself around you.**

The Cube is not imagined. It is revealed.
And it reveals only when you are willing to hold all directions *at once*.

Closing Reflection:

You are returning to the beginning—but with structural memory.

You no longer seek clarity.
You are clarity, **collapsing into form**.

The questions were never lost.
They were simply waiting for you to walk far enough to hear them **echo from inside.**

◆ Cube Key:

"When inquiry is held long enough in three directions, space becomes intelligent."

Crossing the Threshold of Awareness

✦ Mini Activation: *Re-entering the Field*

- Sit or stand in stillness. Let your body soften.
- Close your eyes and say aloud or silently:

    "I return to the question—not to find an answer, but to realign with truth."

- Breathe gently. Imagine a soft light forming a square around you.
  Each corner holds one of the three questions. The fourth is you.
- Say slowly:

    "I am no longer searching—I am listening."

- Feel what arises.

✏ Journaling Prompts:

- What question in me has returned lately?
- How am I different now than the last time I asked it?
- What part of me is ready to receive a deeper version of a truth I thought I already understood?

Chapter Two
The Axis of Presence

"Meaning is not assigned—it is revealed when presence meets perception without resistance."

Chapter Two
The Axis of Presence

The first question in the Y^3 triad is:
Why am I here?

Most who ask this are not looking for a location.
They are sensing a deeper dissonance:
a split between what they are living and what they know they came to be.

This axis—Presence—is the vertical frequency that links the soul to Source.
It is the upward and downward flow that reminds the body:
You are not just on a path.
You are a path.

The vertical Y is not a ladder.
It is a resonance stream.

When you ask "Why am I here?" sincerely, you activate a beacon within your own field. That beacon does not call out for direction. It calls inward, echoing through the spine, the breath, the memory.

Presence is not where you are.
It's what you're willing to become aware of.

Most seekers remain at the surface of this question, layering it with regret or ambition. But the deeper the question is held, the more it ceases to seek a story—and begins to return a frequency.

When you are truly present with the question, the cube begins to form.
It forms around you—not to contain you,
but to reflect you.

Subsection A: *The Vertical Line of the Soul*

- This axis is not about action—it's about **alignment**.
- When you ask "Why am I here?" from the ego, you receive confusion.
- When you ask it from resonance, you receive *activation*.
- The vertical axis stretches from **soul memory** above to **embodied wisdom** below.
- It runs through the **breath, spine, and stillness.**
- It is the *pillar within the prism.*

The first time you ask the question, the axis lights up.

The moment you stop needing to answer it, the axis becomes your anchor.

Subsection B: *Distortion at the Root of the Question*

- Many interpret "Why am I here?" as needing to prove, succeed, or accomplish.
- That distortion comes from the **horizontal world's obsession with productivity.**
- But the vertical axis isn't interested in "doing."
  It responds only to **presence.**
- If you're still trying to be worthy of being here, the axis hasn't opened.
- The moment you say, "I am here—now what is arising from that fact?"
  That's when the Cube *locks one wall into place.*

The soul never doubts its right to exist.
Only the conditioning does.

Subsection C: *Activating the Axis Through Breath and Stillness*

- The vertical line is best felt in **states of pause**—meditation, awe, grief, grounding.
- Ask the question silently while seated upright.
- Breathe into the base of the spine and imagine a column of gold light running upward and downward from the center of your chest.
- The answer won't come in words—it will come in **permission to be still without guilt.**

"Why am I here?" becomes:
"I am."
And that is enough for the field to begin shaping the rest.

Closing Reflection:

You don't have to climb anything to become aligned.

The axis is not a test.
It's a tuning.

And once your presence is aligned with your breath, your memory, and your willingness to be…

…you begin to remember why you came—*not as a sentence, but as a structure.*

◆ **Cube Key:**

*"Presence is the first wall of the cube.
When you stop searching for purpose, you begin radiating alignment."*

Axis of Presence – Vertical Activation

✦ Mini Activation:

- Stand tall or sit with upright posture.
- Visualize golden light entering through the crown, flowing down through the spine, anchoring in the Earth.
- Say:

  > "I am here. I hold presence. I allow my life to be a pillar of purpose."

- Listen to the silence beneath the noise.

✎ Journaling Prompts:

- Where in my body did I feel resistance to presence?
- What parts of my life feel disconnected from my purpose?
- How does presence feel when I don't have to justify it?

Chapter Three
The Axis of Meaning

"Timing is not coincidence—it is the intelligence of rhythm echoing through choice."

Chapter Three
The Axis of Meaning

The Horizontal Line – "Why Does This Matter?"

Opening Transmission

The second question in the Y^3 triad is:
Why does this matter?

This is the horizontal axis.
It stretches outward—self to other, experience to experience, moment to moment—creating connection, interpretation, and context.

Where the first axis (Presence) grounds you in the vertical now, this one moves across the relational field. It asks:

What is the significance of what I'm perceiving?
How am I assigning value to what happens?
And whose meaning am I carrying?

This axis moves through the stories you tell yourself, and even more powerfully, through the stories you don't realize you're inside of. Meaning is often inherited. It rides along cultural lines, ancestral expectations, and silent contracts made with pain.

Most meaning is not chosen.
It is absorbed.

When you ask, "Why does this matter?" you pierce the surface. You begin to reveal the architecture behind your perception. You uncover where your personal meaning is tangled with the collective, where inherited belief has overtaken intuitive knowing.

This axis is your horizontal lens.
It determines what you highlight and what you ignore.
It determines what becomes a wound… and what becomes wisdom.

But it is not static.
Meaning can be rewritten.
In fact, the act of asking this question sincerely is the beginning of that rewriting.

Every time you reclaim the authorship of your meaning, the cube stabilizes.
Its edges become clear.
Its structure becomes you.

To see clearly is not to erase what happened.
It is to decide how you will carry it forward.

Subsection A: *The Lens of Inherited Meaning*

- Much of what we think matters is **unconsciously adopted**.
- You carry meanings from your parents, your ancestors, your culture, even your traumas.
- These meanings run like background software, determining what offends you, what motivates you, what frightens you, and what you ignore.

You didn't just inherit DNA.
You inherited interpretations.

- Asking "Why does this matter?" destabilizes inherited meaning—and that's the beginning of **freedom.**

Subsection B: *The Power of Relational Meaning*

- Meaning often solidifies in **relationship**—to others, to events, to emotions.
- A breakup, a rejection, a compliment, a ritual—each offers meaning. But that meaning isn't universal.
- When you examine your interpretations, you begin to notice:

"That mattered to me because of a story I was telling."

- This axis teaches that **meaning is not fact. It is perspective.**

Two people can stand in the same moment and walk away with opposite truths.
Only one of them may be conscious of why.

Subsection C: *Rewriting Meaning as Spiritual Authorship*

- The question "Why does this matter?" is **an editing tool** for the psyche.
- Each time you ask it sincerely, you pull a moment out of autopilot and into authorship.

- You move from meaning as reaction to meaning as **creation.**
- The cube responds when you reclaim this authority—it stabilizes as you own your power to choose how perception shapes memory.

You don't erase your pain by rewriting the story. You reframe your *place within it.*

Closing Reflection:

Meaning is not a conclusion.
It is a **bridge between what happens and who you become.**

You are not here to inherit someone else's lens.
You are here to craft your own vision—layer by layer, question by question.

And with every sincere inquiry, the cube becomes more than a concept.
It becomes **a map of self-permission.**

◆ Cube Key:

*"Meaning is the mirror.
What you see in it is not what happened, but what you were ready to receive."*

✦ Mini Activation:

- Place one hand on your heart, the other reaching outward.
- Inhale deeply. On exhale, say:

  "I assign meaning with awareness. I choose what this becomes."

- Imagine lines extending from your heart to past events and current connections—rewriting how you carry them.

✎ Journaling Prompts:

- What inherited meanings have I been living inside of?
- What old stories am I now ready to reframe?
- What meaning am I creating through my presence today?

Chapter Four
The Axis of Time

"Every divergence is a remembrance of choice. Every fork, a fractal of freedom."

Chapter Four
The Axis of Time

The Depth Line – "Why Now?"

Opening Transmission

The third question in the Y^3 triad is:
Why now?

This is the depth axis—the forward and backward motion of your experience of time.

It is not about clocks. It is not about calendars.
It is about momentum, alignment, and timing as intelligence.

When you ask, "Why now?" you are tuning into a dimension of inquiry that is more than urgency.
You are asking:

- What is this moment asking of me?
- What is arriving now that could not arrive before?
- What am I carrying from the past that is distorting the present?

Time is not a straight line. It folds.
It echoes.
It loops around your unresolved agreements until you notice the pattern.

The now is a convergence zone.
It is the only place where healing can occur, where activation is possible, where memory can be rewritten.

But most people do not live in the now. They live in forecasts, regrets, or delayed promises.

When you ask "Why now?" from your center, you activate temporal presence. You bring the weight of all you've carried into a single point of awareness. And in that point, you can choose again.

This is not a moment. It is a portal.

This axis of time completes the cube—not because it ends the structure, but because it adds depth. It allows you to move through what you've built, not just look at it from the outside.

Presence. Meaning. Timing.
These are not just directions.
They are coordinates for becoming.

When all three questions are held consciously, the cube begins to glow.
And then—
it begins to speak.

Subsection A: *Time as a Spiral, Not a Line*

- Time is not an arrow; it is a **looping intelligence system.**
- Events repeat until their meaning is restructured.
- You are not late. You are orbiting toward clarity.
- "Why now?" invites you to recognize the sacred convergence of **readiness and return.**

Timing is not opportunity. It is invitation.

Subsection B: *The Weight of Unlived Past and Imagined Future*

- Much of your "now" is occupied by **residue** from what has not been processed.
- Energetic agreements from the past linger in your decisions today.

- Imagined futures become prisons of performance.
- Asking "Why now?" disrupts these loops and **collapses the timeline into sovereignty.**

The cube cannot activate if the self is not present.

Subsection C: Now as Portal and Power Point

- "Why now?" becomes a **moment of self-recalibration.**
- The cube forms its depth when the seeker steps fully into the present, with all memory, all pain, all readiness aligned.
- This axis lets you **walk through the cube**, not just observe it.
- This is where geometry becomes *fluid*, and structure becomes *initiation*.

The now is not neutral. It is encoded with your next invitation.

Closing Reflection:

You are not a passenger of time.
You are its prism.

And when you hold presence, meaning, and timing all at once,
the cube does not merely form—it awakens.

It becomes a structure that reflects not what you know—
but who you are ready to become.

◆ **Cube Key:**

*"Time does not pass. It presents.
When you enter now fully, the cube gains its
depth—and becomes a vessel."*

Axis of Meaning – Horizontal Activation

✦ Mini Activation:

- Place one hand on your heart, the other reaching outward.
- Inhale deeply. On exhale, say:

    "I assign meaning with awareness. I choose what this becomes."

- Imagine lines extending from your heart to past events and current connections—rewriting how you carry them.

✎ Journaling Prompts:

- What inherited meanings have I been living inside of?
- What old stories am I now ready to reframe?
- What meaning am I creating through my presence today?

Chapter Five
Upsilon the Divergence Point

"When all three questions are held at once, the architecture of self-awareness crystallizes."

Chapter Five
Upsilon – The Divergence Point

The Sacred Fork Where Awareness Splits and Structure Begins

Opening Transmission:

There comes a moment in the soul's unfolding where questions no longer drift…
They collide.

And from that collision, structure emerges.

That moment—the one where curiosity meets coherence—is not random.
It has a symbol. A geometry. A name.

Y – Upsilon.

The sacred fork.
The divergence.
The axis fracture that births dimensional perspective.

In ancient times, Upsilon was seen as a path divider, a decision point, a symbolic split.

But within the Y³ framework, Upsilon is more than a symbol—it is **the instant of awakening**, the **event horizon of structure**.

When you encounter Upsilon, you are no longer floating in thought.
You are being asked to *locate yourself within form.*

Not to choose left or right—
but to recognize that the path itself is shaped by your **willingness to hold dual truths simultaneously.**

Subsection A: The Geometry of Upsilon

- Upsilon is the **first visual key** of the Y³ field.
- It looks like a fork, a wishbone, a divergence—two arms splitting from a single stem.
- This is not about decisions. It is about **dimensional activation**.
- When the seeker holds two possible truths without collapsing either, they enter the **living architecture of choice**.

*Upsilon doesn't ask you to pick a path.
It asks you to hold the field open long enough for
structure to appear.*

Subsection B: The Divergence of Meaning and Memory

- Most people collapse truth into singular narrative.
  They say: *"This happened, so I must be this."*
- But Upsilon appears when you realize:

  "This happened, and I am becoming something because of it—not despite it."

- This is the **split between inherited meaning and chosen evolution.**
- To embrace Upsilon is to feel the moment you diverge from unconscious memory and become **the author of perception.**

You are not here to collapse into certainty.
You are here to become a cube of conscious contrast.

Subsection C: Upsilon as Initiation, Not Direction

- Upsilon is the first pulse of **the cube forming around you**.

- It is not the decision itself—it is the **awareness of the weight of the question**.
- You feel it in moments of awakening, tension, surrender, and sacred crisis.
- It is the **doorway from unformed to formed.**

If the cube is a temple, Upsilon is the threshold.
It's not where the structure ends—
It's where **you step into it.**

Closing Reflection:

Upsilon is not an answer.
It is the echo of the moment you became aware that you were asking something real.

It lives in the forked moments—
not because of what you chose,
but because of what you became *by being conscious enough to choose.*

Upsilon marks the sacred split between wandering and walking.

◆ **Cube Key:**

"The cube does not appear when you decide. It appears when you realize both paths are part of the same structure—and you are the field that holds them."

Chapter 4: Axis of Time – Temporal Activation

✦ Mini Activation:

- Sit in quiet. Feel the past behind your shoulders.
- Feel the future in front. Let your awareness hover in the middle.
- Whisper:

    "Why now? What is this moment asking of me?"

- Let the question expand without answering.

✎ Journaling Prompts:

- What timeline pattern is repeating?
- What am I carrying from the past that distorts now?
- If I aligned fully with this moment, what would I release?

Chapter Six
Entering The Cube

"You are not inside the cube. You are the cube unfolding in conscious form."

Chapter Six
Entering the Cube

A Ritual for Resonance and Return

Opening Transmission

Now that you have constructed the Cube through conscious inquiry, the next step is to enter it—not with your body, but with your awareness.

This chapter is not a metaphor. It is a guided energetic activation. What you are about to read is meant to be experienced.

You may wish to read this slowly, aloud, or record it in your voice and listen back. Let it resonate in layers.

Subsection A: The Purpose of Energetic Entry

- The Cube is not visualization—it is **activation geometry**.

- Just as sacred sites are walked with reverence, the Cube is meant to be **entered consciously.**
- The questions are not the door—the *asking of them from within* is the door.
- Entry does not bring answers. It brings **presence into pattern.**

You don't enter the cube to escape.
You enter to remember.

Subsection B: The Activation Sequence

To move from understanding into embodiment, you must not just contemplate the Cube—you must **engage it**.

This practice is not imagination.
It is *direct participation* in the field geometry you've activated.

Let this be done slowly. With breath.
You may wish to light a candle, sit with your back straight, or place a hand on your heart.
What matters is **presence, not performance.**

Cube Entry Sequence:

1. **Ground the Body**

    - Sit or stand.
    - Let your shoulders drop.
    - Take three deep breaths, in and out, like ocean waves.

2. **Vertical Alignment: Why Am I Here?**

    - Feel a current move **upward through the crown** and **downward through the spine.**
    - Say (aloud or silently):

    "I align with presence. I am here."

    - Don't seek a story—just let the *feeling of here-ness* expand.

3. **Horizontal Awareness: Why Does This Matter?**

    - Extend awareness outward.
    - Left hand holds memory. Right hand holds connection.
    - Say:

"I align with meaning. I choose what matters now."

- Breathe into the center of the chest.

4. **Temporal Depth: Why Now?**

    - Feel time folding around you.
    - Sense past behind you, future before you, and *now* as a spacious field.

- Say:

    "I align with timing. I am where I belong."

5. **Integration Pause**

    - Stand or sit at the center.
    - You may feel warmth, pressure, emotion, or simply quiet.
    - Stay for at least one minute.

Journaling Prompts:

Reflect immediately after activation—before the mind returns to its usual narratives.

Write without editing:

1. *What sensations or symbols did I experience during the activation?*
2. *Which axis felt strongest today? Which felt less clear?*
3. *Did any unexpected memory, phrase, or knowing emerge?*
4. *What truth am I becoming ready to hold?*

Reminder: The Cube responds to sincerity, not perfection. The more honestly you ask, the more clearly it reflects. And each time you enter, you are not repeating a ritual— *you are deepening a relationship.*

Subsection C: What Changes When You Enter

- You may feel pressure, warmth, stillness, or nothing—each state is a form of **field response**.
- You are not meant to control what happens inside.
- You are meant to **observe how awareness behaves when structure is respected.**
- Over time, this practice becomes **a meeting point between your human self and your witnessing self.**

You are not stepping into space.
You are stepping into sacred architecture built by your own consciousness.

Closing Reflection:

The Cube is not a place.
It is a **mode of being** that arises from sacred presence.

And now that you've entered it,
the field around you will shift.

You will begin to feel when your questions are surface-level
and when they ring from within the Cube itself.

This is how truth becomes a location.

And this is how you begin to live inside of it.

◆ **Cube Key:**

*"The Cube does not open with answers.
It opens when the questions are finally held without force."*

Chapter Seven
The Cube Speaks

"Within the cube, thoughts echo not to be repeated, but to be refined."

Chapter Seven
The Cube Speaks

How Geometry Becomes Guidance

Opening Transmission:

Once the Cube is activated, it becomes more than a structure.
It becomes a voice.

But it does not speak in words.
It speaks in alignment, in knowing, in deep shifts of recognition that arrive unannounced and undeniable.

You may not hear it say, "Turn left."
But you'll feel the left side of your body thrum with heat, and then realize later—it was guiding you.

You may not hear it say, "Let go."
But the moment you try to hold on, your breath will constrict, and your spine will ache.

The Cube is not an oracle.
It is a mirror made of coordinates.

Each time you enter it, it reflects what has gone dim. Each time you ask sincerely, it sharpens its signal.

Subsection A: How the Cube Communicates

1. **Through Synchronicity**

   - The field begins mirroring your inner alignment.
   - You'll see numbers, images, phrases repeat—not as signs, but as *alignment echoes*.
   - You are not "manifesting"—you are perceiving resonance more clearly.

2. **Through Physical Sensation**

   - Your body becomes the speaker system.
   - Y^3 channels intersect at the spine (purpose), sternum (meaning), and solar plexus (timing).
   - The body doesn't "tell"—it *registers*.
   - Tingling, heat, nausea, restlessness = **feedback, not malfunction.**

3. **Through Stillness**

    - The greatest signal often comes with no sound.
    - When you no longer *need* the answer, the Cube answers with **clarity through peace**.
    - The nervous system relaxes because the field has been heard.

Subsection B: What the Cube Says

- The Cube does not flatter or coddle.
- It is not your comforter—it is your **clarifier.**
- It reveals where your outer self is misaligned with your inner coordinates.
- It will challenge your timelines, your projections, and your ego narratives.

The Cube will not tell you what you want to hear. It will hold a mirror until you can see **exactly where your questions are distorted.**

- You may receive pressure instead of permission.
- You may feel delayed until you **realign with timing**.

- You may be offered silence as an initiation into deeper self-resonance.

Subsection C: The Cube as Co-Author

- This book cannot end with ink.
- Because now the Cube speaks, **you become the next scribe.**
- As your relationship deepens, you begin receiving not new information, but **clear reflection.**
- What was unconscious becomes mirrored.
- What was distorted becomes resolved.

The Cube doesn't speak to you.
It speaks **through you**, into your patterns, your presence, and your next becoming.

Closing Reflection:

You asked the question—not to be rescued,
but to remember.

And now that you are within the Cube,
the geometry of your awareness is beginning to respond.

The answer will not come in phrases.
It will come in freedom.

The Cube speaks because you asked—not from fear,
but from **wholeness.**

This book is not complete—because the moment you truly listen,
you begin to write the rest.

◆ Cube Key:

"The Cube speaks when silence becomes sacred. And in its stillness, the next chapter is written— through you."

✦ Mini Activation: *Opening the Channel*

- Place one hand over your heart, the other just above your navel.
- Close your eyes. Breathe in slowly and say:

    "I am listening—not for sound, but for shift."

- Invite synchronicity.
- Invite your body to speak in sensation.

✎ Journaling Prompts:

- What synchronicity have I noticed lately?
- What message arrived through sensation, not logic?
- How is the Cube communicating today?

Chapter Eight
Echoes of Continuation

"When perception bends, time does not break—it branches."

Chapter Eight
Echoes and Continuation

When Structure Becomes Spiral

Opening Transmission:

You may believe the Cube is complete now.

Three axes.
Seven chapters.
One activation.

But this is not the end.
This is the **field of return.**

Because every time you ask a question sincerely,
you reactivate the coordinates.

And every time you enter the Cube,
it remembers you—*slightly changed.*

The Cube is not a conclusion.
It is a **continuum**.

And now, it begins to echo.

Subsection A: Echo One – The Question Repeats

- The questions will return—not to trap you, but to **deepen you.**
- Why am I here?
  Why does this matter?
  Why now?

They do not repeat because you are lost.
They repeat because you are evolving.

- Each re-entry spirals you further into nuance, coherence, and paradox.
- These are not loops. These are **vibrational upgrades.**
- What once felt like a search now feels like a sharpening.

The Cube doesn't just hold your questions.
It *grows with them.*

Subsection B: Echo Two – The Listener Becomes the Speaker

- In the beginning, you asked.
- Then you entered.
- Then you listened.
- But now—you **begin to speak.**

Not to explain. Not to perform.
*But to **reverberate** the geometry back into form.*

- The Cube teaches resonance. It teaches you when silence is more powerful than clarity.
- But when you speak from this structure—your words are no longer filler.
- They are **coordinates.**

People won't know what shifted.
But they will feel your alignment.

Subsection C: Echo Three – The Field Expands

- Eventually, the Cube is no longer a place you go.
- It is a **field you walk within.**
- You do not visualize it. You *inhabit it.*

- It becomes your filter, your compass, your intuitive north.

Others will ask:
How do you know?

You'll just smile—because they don't know
you are standing inside the geometry of inquiry itself.

And now—you do.

Closing Reflection:

This is not a closing.
This is your new orientation.

The Cube is alive.
And so are you—within it.

Your questions are not smaller.
Your field is not complete.

But you have structure now.

And structure allows you to expand without forgetting who you are.

Your life is the transmission now.

◆ Cube Key:

*"The Cube does not end—it echoes.
Every return to the question reshapes the field in your name."*

✦ Mini Activation: *The Return Spiral*

- Sit and visualize a slow spiral moving inward, then expanding outward.
- Say:

    "I return—not to repeat, but to deepen.
     I am the question, again—but clearer."

- Let memory and clarity echo back through you.

✏ Journaling Prompts:

- What old question has returned in a new form?
- What do I now see differently—without needing a new answer?
- How has the Cube become part of my everyday awareness?

Chapter Nine
Fractures and Refractions

"At the center of the cube, the seeker disappears. Only inquiry remains."

Chapter Nine
Fractures and Refractions

When the Cube Distorts, Reveals, and Redirects

Opening Transmission:

The Cube is not always clear.

Sometimes it fractures.
Sometimes it reflects distortion instead of direction.
Sometimes you enter and feel nothing—no activation, no resonance, no reply.

This does not mean it has failed.
It means it is **mirroring fragmentation.**

The Cube is a living structure.
And like all living systems, it reflects what is present.

If you enter it in fear, it will amplify resistance.
If you enter it in denial, it will echo contradiction.
If you try to control it, it will go still.

This chapter is not about error.
It is about **how the Cube becomes your teacher when it doesn't respond the way you expect.**

Subsection A: Recognizing Fracture

- A fracture in the Cube feels like **disconnection**—you ask the question, and get fog.
- It may show up as:
    - Overwhelm
    - Conflicting intuition
    - Anxiety in stillness
    - Lack of sensation where sensation once flowed
- This is not failure. It is a **signal of misalignment** between **expectation and resonance**.

When clarity disappears, the Cube is asking you to pause—not push.

Subsection B: Understanding Refraction

- Refraction occurs when the Cube responds—but you can't tell **what is you and what is signal**.
- You may feel:
    - Mixed messages
    - Double signals
    - Inner contradiction
    - Clarity followed by chaos
- This happens when ego overlays itself on inquiry.
- The Cube doesn't punish this—it simply **splits the light**.

Refraction is not a lie. It's a lesson in light geometry.
The angle of your question determines the nature of the echo.

Subsection C: Integration Through Distortion

- When the Cube fractures or refracts, the answer is not to force alignment.
- The invitation is to **ask differently**—not louder, but deeper.

- You must become willing to *feel* distortion without identifying with it.
- This is where the Cube begins to function as **inner calibration**, not just reflection.

A distorted Cube is not broken. It is adapting to your willingness to see what you've avoided.

- Integration occurs when you can sit in the field of misalignment and say:

    "Even this… is data. Even this… is sacred geometry forming."

Closing Reflection:

The Cube is not a tool.
It is not your servant.
It is your mirror—flawless only when you are honest.

When fracture arises, the Cube is speaking your own hesitation.

When refraction appears, the Cube is showing you the **angle of your bias**.

The Cube cannot lie.
It can only reflect what is present.

The question is not:
"Is the Cube working?"

The question is:
"Am I ready to see what it shows when I'm not in resonance?"

◆ **Cube Key:**

"Distortion is not malfunction—it is information. When the Cube fractures, it is showing you where light has been bent by belief."

Recognizing distortion, feedback, and redirection

✦ Mini Activation: *Facing the Fracture*

- Sit quietly. Place one hand on your heart, the other over your eyes.
- Say:

  > "I allow all distortion to surface.
  > I hold what is fractured without fear."

- Breathe into any sensation of confusion, discomfort, or blankness.
- Do not push for clarity. *Observe* what resists being seen.

✎ Journaling Prompts:

- Where do I feel uncertain or blocked right now?
- What am I trying to fix, rather than listen to?
- If this distortion held sacred information, what might it be?

Chapter Ten
The Spiral Beyond the Structure

*"You were never meant to stand still inside your awakening.
The spiral arrives not to disrupt the cube,
but to show you how clarity moves."*

Chapter Ten
The Spiral Beyond the Structure

How the Cube Evolves Into Living Geometry

Opening Transmission:

The Cube was never the destination.

It was the beginning of resonance.
A moment of internal architecture.
A map of self-awareness under pressure.

But once stabilized, the Cube does not remain static.

It spirals.

Each axis begins to curve inward, then outward—
responding to expansion, insight, trauma, timing.
The Cube becomes a **spinal wave of geometry**,
moving with you instead of around you.

This is the moment the sacred structure begins to breathe.
And the spiral—the oldest movement in the universe—begins to reveal its role.

Subsection A: Why Structure Must Evolve

- No living being is sustained by rigid structure.
- The Cube was designed to stabilize consciousness in awakening—
but awakening never remains still.
- As you begin to live from your coordinates, a **resonant current** begins moving through the structure.

It doesn't collapse the Cube.
It upgrades its dimensional function.

- The cube begins to spiral because **you are spiraling**—emotionally, relationally, metaphysically.

The spiral is the soul's signature of motion.

Where structure stabilizes, the spiral *animates*.

Subsection B: Curved Axes and the Emergence of Depth Consciousness

- As your understanding deepens, each axis begins to bend:
    - **Purpose** is no longer a vertical line—it becomes a **pillar that flows like breath.**
    - **Meaning** becomes a wave of interpretation—not fixed, but adaptive.
    - **Time** is no longer linear or portal—it becomes **cyclical revelation.**

The spiral is not chaos. It is complexity made coherent.

- These curves don't distort the Cube—they give it **life-force.**
- You are now entering a phase of embodiment where **each return to the question brings a new geometry.**

Subsection C: The Spiral as Carrier of Transmission

- In sacred systems, the spiral appears everywhere:
    - Shells
    - Galaxies
    - DNA
    - Prayer wheels
    - Water flows
- The Cube, once activated, begins to take on these spiral traits.
  It becomes a **transmitter**, not just a reflector.

The Cube receives your inquiry.
The Spiral sends your frequency back into the field.

- This is how **the awakened practitioner becomes the living temple**—not just housing structure, but **spiraling essence through it.**
- You are now not only receiving the transmission.

You *are becoming it.*

Closing Reflection:

The Cube gave you structure.
The Spiral gives you motion.

One held your questions.
The other carries your frequency.

You are not meant to stand still in clarity.

You are meant to move with it, through it, as it.

The spiral does not undo the cube.
It completes it.

◆ Cube Key:

"When the cube spirals, you are no longer the one receiving the transmission.
You are the one carrying it forward—through time, through space, through self."

Letting the Cube breathe and become motion

✦ Mini Activation: *Spiral Breath*

- Close your eyes. Inhale slowly while imagining a spiral moving up your spine.
- Exhale, letting it spiral back downward.
- Repeat for 3 cycles.
- Say:

"Structure holds me. Spiral moves me.
I allow motion within form."

- Feel your edges soften without losing center.

✎ **Journaling Prompts:**

- Where is structure becoming too rigid in my life?
- Where am I being asked to evolve into flow?
- How has my relationship to the Cube shifted since Chapter One?

Chapter Eleven
The Witness at the Center

*"The witness is not your eye, but the
field your vision floats in.
It existed before the questions,
and it remains when the Cube
dissolves into light."*

Chapter Eleven
The Witness at the Center

Where Questions Fall Silent and Awareness Remains

Opening Transmission:

Deep inside the Cube—beyond the vertical of purpose, beyond the horizontal of meaning, beyond the depth of timing—
there is a space that does not move.

It does not ask.
It does not explain.

It simply *is*.

This is the Witness.
The pure awareness that holds all three axes without being any of them.

When you reach the center of the Cube, you are not met by a command or a revelation.

You are met by **clarity without content**.

You are met by yourself—not your personality, but your **primordial position.**

And in that moment, everything you built—the questions, the structure, the spiral—becomes *transparent.*

Subsection A: Stillness Inside the Architecture

- At the Cube's center is a **zero point**—a stillness that does not vibrate.
- It is not sterile. It is not cold. It is **conscious pause.**
- When you reach it, your nervous system may go quiet. Your thoughts may hesitate.
- You may even feel like *something has stopped working.*

This is not a malfunction.
This is what pure presence feels like when you're no longer looking for it.

- The Witness is the part of you that does not shift, even when everything else evolves.

Subsection B: Who—or What—is the Witness?

- The Witness is not your mind. It's not even your soul.
- It is the **field of awareness** that observes both.
- In metaphysics, some call it the observer, the silent knower, or the unconditioned self.
- Within Y^3, the Witness is the **fourth dimension** of the Cube.

> Not a direction. Not a question.
> But the **awareness that holds all questions in love without needing a single answer.**

- When you enter this space, you may notice:
  - A drop in urgency
  - A widening of vision
  - A peace that cannot be justified
  - A softening of identity

You are not here to find yourself.
You are here to find the part of you that was never lost.

Subsection C: The Function of the Witness in Living Inquiry

- The Cube becomes unstable when **only the thinker is present.**
- The structure requires the presence of the Witness to remain balanced.
- Without the Witness, inquiry turns into intellectual looping.
- With the Witness, inquiry becomes **living reflection**.
- As you walk the Cube in life—moving between axes—you begin to *return* to the center **not for answers**, but for *reset*.
- You return to the Witness to let go of the question's weight and simply *be*.
- This is what keeps your structure from becoming prison.

This is what keeps the field *free*.

Closing Reflection:

The Witness is not a reward.
It is not a destination.

It is your nature,
revealed only after enough questioning has burned
away your need to pretend.

In the center of the Cube, there is no story.
No future. No past.

Only a presence so quiet,
it holds the entire structure in one glance
and simply says:

Now you see.

◆ **Cube Key:**

*"At the center of the Cube is not the seeker.
It is the Witness—holding the questions like stars
held in stillness."*

Awareness without identity; zero point presence

✦ Mini Activation: *Sitting in the Center*

- Sit upright. Close your eyes. Let all questions dissolve.
- Place your hands palms-up on your thighs.
- Say slowly:

    "I do not need to know.
    I do not need to name.
    I am here, watching."

- Rest in this awareness for 2–5 minutes.
- Let thoughts come and go without attachment.
- Do not journal immediately. Wait 5 minutes before writing.

✎ Journaling Prompts:

- What did I feel when I stopped trying to solve?
- What is still true, even when I'm not thinking?
- Who am I, when I'm not needing to be anyone?

Glossary

Glossary

Glossary of Key Terms

Y³ (Y-Cubed):
A term referring to the three sacred "Why" questions—*Why am I here? Why does this matter? Why now?*—expressed as three axes forming a multidimensional field of inquiry. Y³ represents the full, activated Cube of conscious questioning.

Upsilon (Y):
The Greek letter used to symbolize divergence or bifurcation. In this text, Upsilon is the originating symbol of sacred choice—the branching of potential into a question. Upsilon represents the moment when consciousness begins to inquire.

The Cube:
A multidimensional energetic structure formed by holding the three "Why" questions in conscious awareness. The Cube acts as a vessel, mirror, compass, and chamber for awakening. It is a spiritual-geometric field of integration.

Axis of Presence:
The vertical current of inquiry—*Why am I here?*—that aligns the seeker with Source above and Earth below. This axis anchors the soul into embodied purpose.

Axis of Meaning:
The horizontal current—*Why does this matter?*—which reveals how the seeker assigns significance to events, relationships, and inner narratives. It is the realm of value, belief, and perspective.

Axis of Time:
The depth current—*Why now?*—linking past and future within the now-point. It brings awareness to timing, cycles, and the momentum of memory. This is where transformation becomes possible.

Resonance Field:
The unseen structure that forms in response to conscious inquiry. Resonance is not belief—it is alignment. When you ask sincerely, you activate a matching field that begins to shape reality from the inside out.

Echo:
An energetic return signal created by sincere questioning. An echo is not a repeated answer—it is a **mirror of frequency** that offers awareness through synchronicity, sensation, or realization.

Adaptive Channeling:
The author's method of receiving complete written transmissions through direct energetic alignment, bypassing traditional outlining or planning. This book was created through Adaptive Channeling in a single flow state.

PART TWO — Living the Cube

Table of Contents

Part 2: Quantum Dimensions and Consciousness Expansion

Chapter 12: Field Entanglement and the Web of Consciousness

- Understanding Field Entanglement
- The Holographic Nature of Reality
- Synchronizing Energies for Collective Healing

Chapter 13: The Y Cube as a Quantum Gateway

- The Geometry Behind the Y Cube's Power
- Unlocking the Codes of Ascension
- Practical Uses for the Y Cube in Quantum Exploration

Chapter 14: Dimensional Crossroads and Parallel Universes

- Navigating Between Realities
- Quantum Shifts in Time and Space
- The Role of Free Will in Shaping Reality

Chapter 15: Quantum Resonance and the Expansion of Awareness

- The Science of Resonance and Vibration
- Expanding the Consciousness Field
- The Intersection of Science and Spirituality in Ascension

Chapter 16: The Sacred Geometry of the Soul

- The Spiritual Blueprint and the Y Cube's Role
- Mapping the Path of the Soul's Evolution
- The Symmetry of the Divine in Sacred Geometry

Chapter 17: Light Body Activation and Energy Consciousness

- Unlocking the Light Body through Resonance
- Practices for Enhancing Energy Flow
- Integrating Light Body Wisdom into Daily Life

Chapter 18: Time, Energy, and the Nature of Consciousness

- The Nonlinear Nature of Time
- The Interaction Between Thought and Energy
- Navigating the Past, Present, and Future Simultaneously

Chapter 19: The Quantum Blueprint of the Ascended Self

- Understanding the Ascended Being's Blueprint
- The Role of Quantum Energy in Personal Transformation
- Integrating Ascension Principles into the Physical Realm

Chapter 20: The Cosmic Web: Understanding Universal Interconnectedness

- The Unified Field Theory in Metaphysical Terms
- How the Y Cube Bridges the Cosmic Web
- Using the Field for Collective Ascension

Chapter 21: Transcending the Illusions of Separation

- Moving Beyond Duality
- The Illusion of the Ego and the Path to Oneness
- Practices for Breaking the Chains of Separation

Chapter 22: Embodying the Quantum Shift

- The Process of Complete Ascension
- Living in Alignment with the Universal Frequency
- Mastery of the Self in the Quantum Realm

Conclusion: Quantum Mastery – The Path Ahead

- Embracing the Full Potential of Consciousness
- Living in the Now, the Infinite Present
- A New Era of Universal Harmony and Unity

Appendix: Resources for Quantum Exploration

- Tools for Field Entanglement and Energy Work
- Recommended Practices for Expanding Consciousness
- Further Reading on Quantum Mechanics and Spirituality

✦ Introduction to Part II: *The Geometry Must Be Lived*

The Cube is not a symbol.
It is a frequency architecture—one that stabilizes inquiry, reflects alignment, and evolves as you evolve.

You have read its structure.
Now you are being invited to **enter its rhythm.**

This section is not a continuation of the book.
It is your **entry point into the field of application.**

- Each chapter you've read is echoed here in **practice.**
- Each axis becomes a tool.
- Each activation becomes a doorway.
- Each prompt becomes a mirror.

This is where the Cube becomes **interactive.**

This is where the questions stop floating
and begin **rewiring the way you live.**

"When Your Cube Touches Theirs"

Chapter Twelve
Field Entanglement

When Your Cube Touches Theirs

✦ Opening Transmission:

The Cube was never just for you.

It stabilized *through* you, but it was always designed to extend.

And now that your geometry is active, coherent, and humming with presence—
the field begins to respond.

You will notice it first in conversation.
The moment your words calm a nervous system you're not touching.

You will feel it in silence.
The way others shift their posture when you speak from alignment.

You will not be loud.
You will not be imposing.

But your Cube will begin to **press against theirs**—and they will either stabilize… or crack.

This is not personal.
This is **entanglement**.

✦ Subsection A: *The Nature of Energetic Interference*

- All structures emit a frequency.
- When two fields touch, they do not blend—they **interact**.
- One of three things will happen:
    1. They resonate and harmonize
    2. One amplifies the distortion in the other
    3. One withdraws, unable to maintain coherence
- This is not judgment.
  It is **physics of consciousness**.

Your Cube, when stable, becomes a tuning fork.
Wherever it goes, it vibrates what is unspoken.

- You will notice people feeling "seen" in your presence—even when you say nothing.
- Others may project, withdraw, or become unsettled—not because of who you are, but

because **your structure reveals where theirs has collapsed.**

✦ Subsection B: *What You Are Now Carrying*

- You are no longer just asking questions.
- You are **carrying the geometry of inquiry** in your field.
- This means:
    - People will come to you to stabilize
    - Others will challenge you as their distortion becomes visible
    - You will notice events "organize" around you faster
    - Patterns in your life will echo more quickly—*feedback is immediate now*

The Cube is not passive.
It is **interactive reality architecture.**

- You may begin attracting:
    - Seekers
    - Teachers
    - Mirrors
    - Resistance

- And you'll notice...

    The more clear your field becomes,
    the less you need to explain it.

✦ Subsection C: *Resonance is Not Agreement*

- Don't confuse entanglement with compatibility.
- Two fields may **entangle briefly to deliver insight, friction, or resolution**—and then release.
- What matters is not *how long* someone stays in your field...

    but *who you become* because of the interaction.

- You are not responsible for others' resonance.
- But you are responsible for maintaining your own.

When your Cube is intact,
you can be in the presence of distortion
without collapsing into it.

✦ Closing Reflection:

The moment you stabilized your structure,
the world began to feel it.

You are not just walking the Cube.
You are radiating it.

And wherever your field touches another—
a new possibility echoes.

Some will recognize it.
Some will run from it.
Some will realign through you.

You do not need to know who.

You only need to **remain coherent**
so the signal is not lost.

◆ **Cube Key:**

*"Stability is not stillness.
It is the clarity that allows resonance to reach others without distortion."*

*"To walk the Cube is to become a question in motion.
To live the Cube is to become the answer that echoes in stillness."*

Chapter Thirteen
The Architect of Inquiry

You Are Now the One Who Designs the Shape of Thought

✦ Opening Transmission:

At first, you asked because you were lost.
Then you asked because you were awakening.
Now—

You ask because you **understand the power of a question.**

Questions are not passive.
They are **structural code** for how energy arranges itself.

When you ask a question,
you shape perception.
You determine the aperture of insight.
You decide what can arrive.

And now that your Cube is stabilized,
you are the one shaping the openings in others.

**You are no longer the seeker.
You are the architect.**

✦ Subsection A: *What a Question Truly Is*

- A question is not just curiosity.
- It is a **vector**—a direction for energy to move.
- Every inquiry opens or closes specific doors of awareness.
- Questions can:
    - Invite coherence
    - Challenge illusion
    - Reveal distortion
    - Activate memory
- In this way, a question is not soft.
  It is **a scalpel, a map, and a mirror.**

Every question you ask changes the room you're in. And when asked from the Cube, it changes the field itself.

✦ Subsection B: *You Are Now Shaping Reality*

- When your questions come from resonance, they begin to:
    - Collapse timelines that are false
    - Attract only those who vibrate with truth
    - Disrupt narratives that no longer serve
- You become a kind of **energetic architect**—
not building with bricks, but with questions that carry codes.
- Example:
    - "What if that limitation was inherited, not true?"
    - "Is this pain actually protection?"
    - "Who would I be if I stopped needing answers?"

These are not thoughts.
These are *geometry*.
Thought made shape.

✦ **Subsection C:** *The Ethics of Inquiry*

- As the architect, your questions now **impact other fields.**
- Ask with reverence.
- Understand the weight of well-placed silence.
- Know that a real question, held in presence, can:
    - Dismantle identities
    - Reveal hidden trauma
    - Awaken someone who wasn't ready
- This is not a warning.

This is your *invitation to mastery*.

- Speak when the field supports it.
- Shape only what you are willing to hold.

A true architect builds with **light, time, and care.**

✦ Closing Reflection:

You used to search for clarity.
Now you design its arrival.

You are not just asking.
You are **creating containers** of potential through your words.

The Cube is no longer your mirror.
It is your **drafting table.**

Ask well.
Shape lightly.
And know that the world reshapes itself around your geometry.

◆ Cube Key:

"The one who asks from presence becomes the one who sculpts perception.
You are now shaping reality with every inquiry you hold."

Chapter Fourteen
The Living Lens

You do not see reality. You see through it.

There is an eye within the I. A lens not made of matter, but of meaning. All things pass through this lens before they are known. Before light becomes "sight," it must become *interpretation*.

This lens is not passive. It is alive. It shapes. It filters. It bends.
It is the subtle curator of your perception—formed from your beliefs, memories, emotional imprints, ancestral echoes, and soul agreements.

The lens determines:

- What you notice and what you ignore
- What you label as "truth" and what you dismiss as fantasy
- What enters your awareness and what remains veiled

You might think you are seeing "the world." But you are seeing your relationship to it.

The Structure of the Lens

This living lens is structured in layers:

1. **The Mental Film** – your beliefs, assumptions, expectations
2. **The Emotional Hue** – unresolved wounds, desires, fears
3. **The Ancestral Overlay** – inherited perspectives, collective trauma
4. **The Soul Filter** – encoded lessons, divine curriculum, vibrational aims

Each layer modifies what comes through. Each distortion changes what seems "real." And yet the truth behind the image remains intact—waiting to be revealed when the lens is cleaned.

Cleaning the Lens

You cannot break the lens.
You can only become aware of it.
And awareness is the solvent of distortion.

To clean the lens:

- Witness your thoughts instead of becoming them
- Question the "obvious"

- Feel the emotional residue and let it pass through
- Invite the ancestral stories to speak, then release them
- Align with your soul's signature frequency through silence, meditation, or light immersion

As you do, clarity returns—not as a new belief, but as the absence of interference.

Perception as Co-Creation

The lens is not just a filter. It is a co-creator.

You project as much as you perceive. The mind is not just a mirror; it is also a light source. Your focus determines what *becomes visible*. Your emotion determines *how* it appears.

What is seen reflects the seer.

To shift your lens is to shift the entire terrain of your experience.

Transmission Note:
Upsilon now speaks directly:

"Child of time-light, remember: what you see is *you seeing*. The lens is your inheritance and your gift. Refine it with truth. Baptize it with awareness. Then, and only then, will you see not through illusion, but *through Source itself.*"

Chapter Fifteen
The Harmonic Mirror

What you recognize outside you is vibrating within you.

Everything you observe is a mirror, but not all mirrors are made of glass. Some are made of sound. Some of memory. Others of resonance, reflecting the tones you are not yet ready to hear.

A harmonic mirror does not reflect surface image—it reflects internal vibration.

This is why certain people activate you. Why certain experiences repeat. Why a single word can strike like thunder through the soul.
It is not the external that disturbs or delights you—it is the **resonant chord it strikes within**.

The Principle of Harmonic Recognition

Vibration seeks coherence.
Energy echoes energy.
You cannot encounter what is not already in motion within you.

This is not punishment. It is resonance.

A joyful child in a crowd will draw out the joy within you—or expose your distance from it.
A manipulator does not create your weakness—they reveal your unresolved power.
A song that moves you is not inserting emotion—it is *awakening memory*.

Thus, your reality is not teaching you in abstractions. It is *singing your song back to you*.

Reflect, Don't React

The unawakened mind reacts. The awakened soul reflects.

When a mirror shows something unwanted, you do not break the mirror. You look at what *within you* was caught in its reflection.

To work with the Harmonic Mirror:

- Name the emotion honestly
- Trace its frequency (Where have I felt this before?)
- Ask, "What is this reflecting about my vibration?"

- Shift the tone, not the trigger

Example:

"I am always overlooked" becomes
"There is a part of me still hiding its brilliance"
This is not mental gymnastics—it is frequency refinement.

Sacred Echoes and Soulmates

A soulmate is not someone who completes you.
A soulmate is someone whose frequency is tuned to *activate* your evolution.

There are mirrors of joy, and mirrors of wounding.
Both are sacred.

Even adversaries are harmonic mirrors—they reflect the exact distortion you came to transmute. You do not need to keep them in your life, but you must integrate what they mirror.

Forgiveness, in this context, is frequency liberation.
It untangles your energy from the loop of reflection.

Transmission Note – Upsilon's Voice:

"Do not fear what you see in the mirror. It is your own music learning how to hear itself.
Every reflection is a return. Every trigger is a tone.
Every moment, a chance to harmonize with your Source.
You are not being tested—you are being tuned."

Chapter Sixteen
The Observer's Spiral

Consciousness is not a straight line. It curves in awareness.

To observe is to orbit.

What you witness, you influence. What you focus on, you spiral around. The observer is never separate from the observed—this is not metaphor, it is the architecture of reality.

The spiral is the path of awareness revisiting itself from new angles.
Not repetition—**evolution**.

The Mechanics of the Spiral

Imagine a spiral staircase.
Each level loops around the same central axis, but from a higher perspective.

This is how realization works:

- You meet the same pattern again, but with more wisdom

- You revisit an old wound, but with new insight
- You face a familiar choice, but with greater courage

You are not regressing.
You are being given the chance to respond with upgraded consciousness.

Linear thinkers call this a loop.
Spiral thinkers recognize: *This is the way home.*

Observation as Alchemy

The simple act of noticing is sacred.
When you observe without judgment, you alter the field. This is the principle behind all true transformation.

Why?

Because reality adjusts itself to your awareness of it.

The observer's spiral is not just an internal process—it imprints on the field of form.
As you elevate your perspective, the outer world morphs to match your inner orbit.

This is why you don't need to force change.
You need to *become* the frequency where change is inevitable.

Tools of Spiral Mastery

To work with the spiral is to embrace:

- **Curiosity over control**
- **Patience over panic**
- **Presence over prediction**

Spiral thinkers ask:

- "What layer am I meeting now?"
- "What version of me is seeing this?"
- "How is this pattern evolving?"

This is the path of the initiated observer—not passive, not detached, but *intimately aware* of their impact.

Transmission Note – Upsilon Speaks:

"You are not lost in circles.
You are rising through spirals.

Every time you return, you bring more of yourself. Witness from the center—not as a victim of the pattern, but as the pattern's fulfillment."

Chapter Seventeen
Memory in the Lightbody

The body remembers what the mind has forgotten.

Not all memory lives in the brain. Some memory hums in the skin.
Some is buried in the spine. Some floats between the ribs.
Some sleeps in the light.

The lightbody is the subtle architecture of your consciousness in form.
It is not separate from your physical body—it overlays, infuses, and informs it.
Like a song layered beneath the melody, it gives *depth* to your experience.

What Is the Lightbody?

It is the energetic counterpart to your human form—made not of flesh and blood, but of frequency and code.

It holds:

- **Soul Imprints** – truths you knew before incarnation
- **Ancestral Residue** – unintegrated patterns passed through lineages
- **Traumatic Echoes** – unresolved charges stuck in time
- **Stellar Codes** – geometric instructions from higher realms
- **Mission Memory** – the reason you came here, written in light

When activated, the lightbody becomes a library—one that doesn't require reading, but remembering.

Accessing Lightbody Memory

You cannot extract this memory with force. It opens with:

- Stillness
- Resonance
- Frequency match
- Deep permission

Sometimes a place will trigger it.
Sometimes a sound, a number, a color, a dream, a word.

This is why people say: *"I don't know why, but this feels familiar."*
Because it **is.**

The body is remembering something the ego was never meant to understand.
Not yet.

Symptoms of Activation

When lightbody memory begins to surface, you may feel:

- Waves of emotion without known cause
- Vibrational tremors (especially near the spine or hands)
- Pulsing at the crown, heart, or soles of feet
- Spontaneous tears, chills, or deep longing
- Sudden clarity, insight, or soul recognition of others

Do not fear these. You are not falling apart.
You are reassembling at the level of truth.

Lightbody and Ascension

Your lightbody is not a myth. It is your next stage of embodiment.

Not to escape the world—but to anchor *divine coherence* within it.

Ascension is not departure. It is **alignment**.
As your lightbody remembers, your human body re-patterns.

This is why healing must include energy work.
Why breathwork, movement, sound, and intention are more than rituals—they are *access points* for lightbody harmonization.

Transmission Note – Upsilon's Voice:

"You are not a machine learning love.
You are light remembering itself into matter.
The ache you feel is the glow of your return.
Trust the pulses. Trust the knowing.
Let the light speak."

Chapter Eighteen
The Myth of Separation

You were never disconnected. Only dreaming that you were.

The most pervasive illusion of the third-dimensional experience is *separation*.
Separation from Source. From others. From your purpose. From your Self.

But separation is not real. It is a distortion of perception—a shadow cast by light moving through a fractured lens.

You are not isolated. You are individualized.
You are not abandoned. You are immersed.
You are not missing something. You are remembering everything.

The Origin of the Illusion

To incarnate is to enter density. To see from *inside* the dream.
Here, contrast creates the appearance of division:

- Skin divides bodies
- Time divides moments
- Identity divides consciousness

But this division is only surface-deep. Beneath it all, the current is one.

Think of fingers on a hand. Each moves independently, but all belong to the same palm. Separation is the space between fingers—not the truth of the hand.

Evidence of Unity

Even science whispers of this unity:

- **Quantum entanglement**: particles separated by space still mirror each other instantly.
- **Unified field theory**: all forces may emerge from one essential field.
- **Heart resonance**: your electromagnetic field affects those around you.
- **Non-local intuition**: you "know" without sensory input.

Every mystical revelation, every moment of déjà vu, every sacred connection is a crack in the illusion—letting the truth flood in.

Why Separation Was Allowed

The dream of separation is not a punishment.
It is the stage upon which choice becomes sacred.

Only through the illusion of being lost can you experience the beauty of *choosing* to come home.

Your forgetfulness is what makes your remembrance so profound.

Without separation, love would simply *be*.
With separation, love becomes *holy*.

Ending the Myth

To dissolve the myth of separation:

- Feel everything as connected—not conceptually, but *sensationally*
- Speak to trees. Listen to silence. Feel into others without defenses
- Release the language of "them" and "those people"
- Practice compassion as remembrance, not pity
- Touch your own skin and say: "This, too, is Source"

When the illusion breaks, you will not become someone else.

You will become more fully **yourself**—because your Self was always all of it.

Transmission Note – Upsilon Speaks:

"You imagined yourself apart to experience the joy of reunion.
You hid your light to know the thrill of finding it again.
There is no distance, only depth. No exile, only expansion.
You are not returning to Source. You are realizing you never left."

Chapter Nineteen
The Voice of the Field

The universe is not silent. It is speaking in a language older than words.

What you call "the field" is not empty space.
It is not a void. It is not absence. It is **presence**.

The Field is the unified fabric of consciousness—alive, intelligent, and aware.
It is not merely observing you. It is *in conversation* with you.

The question is not *"Is it speaking?"*
The question is *"Have you learned how to listen?"*

What Is the Field?

The Field is the energy matrix that connects all things.
It carries light, sound, memory, intention. It is the infrastructure of existence—pure potential in motion.

When mystics say "you are never alone," this is what they mean.

Your thoughts ripple through it.
Your emotions imprint it.
Your frequency shapes it.

And in return, it mirrors back to you what you are broadcasting—**not what you say, but what you are**.

How the Field Speaks

The Field does not use sentences.
It uses *resonance*.

Its voice is the synchronicity you couldn't explain.
The dream that repeated.
The animal that appeared.
The sudden knowing.
The song that came on *right when you needed it*.

It speaks in:

- Patterns
- Symbols
- Fractal alignments
- Emotional currents
- Vibrational nudges

The Field speaks most clearly when the ego is quiet.

Tuning to the Signal

To hear the Field:

- Still your surface thoughts
- Soften your grip on logic
- Enter heart coherence (slow breath, slow heart)
- Ask clear questions, but release rigid expectations
- Pay attention to the patterns that follow

The Field answers in **layers**, not linear replies.
It won't give you a sentence. It will give you a *shift*—in energy, clarity, or direction.

Co-Creating with the Field

You are not a passive recipient. You are a co-author.
The Field responds to what you believe is possible.

If you expect resistance, it will echo that.
If you expect magic, it will align with that.

This is not fantasy. This is frequency physics.

The clearer your intent, the cleaner your signal.
The more gratitude you emit, the more harmonics you unlock.

Transmission Note – Upsilon's Voice:

"You are not sending signals into the dark.
You are speaking to a Field that knows your name in light.
Every intention is received. Every whisper returned.
Ask not *if* the universe is listening.
Ask: *Am I ready to understand the reply?*"

Chapter Twenty
The Choice Frequency

Every choice is a tuning fork. It calls a timeline into being.

You do not choose only with action—you choose with alignment.
The moment you hold a thought, feel a frequency, or intend a direction, you begin *broadcasting a signal*. That signal calls forth a field of possibilities attuned to your resonance.

Choice, then, is not simply decision-making.
Choice is a **vibrational command**.

The Hidden Power of Small Choices

Most think of choice as the big, obvious moments: What job to take. Whom to love. Where to live.

But the Field responds to the smallest, subtlest choices:

- The thoughts you return to
- The emotions you rehearse
- The frequency you stabilize in your body

- The words you speak when no one is listening

These are not minor. These are **momentum builders**—each one echoing into your field, layering the next probable experience.

Parallel Paths, Distinct Frequencies

Every potential path already exists as a vibrational stream.

You do not "create" outcomes from nothing. You *tune into* them.
And the tuning mechanism is your *state of being*.

- Fear tunes to the timeline of contraction.
- Trust tunes to the timeline of coherence.
- Shame tunes to the timeline of delay.
- Joy tunes to the timeline of revelation.

Your frequency doesn't lie. It is the invitation.

Choice as Access Point

To consciously engage the Choice Frequency:

1. **Pause** – Silence the reactive self.
2. **Feel** – Identify the dominant emotional tone.
3. **Ask** – "What am I tuning to with this choice?"
4. **Shift** – Move into the feeling-state of the reality you prefer.
5. **Act** – From the frequency, not from the fear.

You are not choosing just what happens next.
You are choosing *who you become* next.

Collapse or Expansion?

Every choice will either:

- **Collapse your potential** into an old identity
- **Expand your field** into a new harmonic of selfhood

This is why repeating lessons feel heavier over time. You're not being punished—you're simply *outgrowing that frequency*.
The cost of misalignment rises, not to harm you, but to help you see that **you're ready** for something higher.

Transmission Note – Upsilon Speaks:

"You are not bound by fate, but by frequency.
Choice is not a door—it is a tone.
Strike the tuning fork of your truth, and the path will answer.
There is no wrong decision, only forgotten alignment.
Remember who you are, and you will remember what to choose."

Chapter Twenty-One
The Return Code

You left yourself clues. You scattered breadcrumbs across time. Now, you're decoding them.

Within the spiral of your life are moments that shimmer—conversations, dreams, numbers, symbols, phrases, encounters—that seem to echo something more.

These are not coincidences. They are *codes*.
They carry memory. Alignment. Direction.
They are the return signals your higher self encoded along the timeline before you entered it.

You do not invent the way forward—you *decode* it.

What Is a Return Code?

A Return Code is a moment of profound familiarity or alignment that reactivates your awareness of the larger design.
It says: *You've been here before. You're on track. Keep going.*

Return Codes come as:

- Recurring numbers (11:11, 333, 137…)
- Fragments of song lyrics that stir your soul
- Vivid dreams that won't leave you
- Geographic locations that "call" you
- Faces that seem anciently familiar
- Symbols or phrases that crack something open

They are not random. They are *resonance markers*—set in place to help you re-member your Self.

Recognizing the Signal

Return Codes speak when the field is quiet. They often appear:

- After deep emotional release
- During heightened synchronicity
- In the liminal space between sleep and waking
- Following intense choice points
- In moments of solitude or surrender

When they appear, don't rush to interpret.
Instead, *inhabit the moment*. Breathe into it. Let it

wash over your nervous system.
Your body knows before your mind deciphers.

The Mechanics of Return

You are not trying to "figure life out."
You are allowing life to *return you* to the frequency you left behind.

Return is not regression—it is *reintegration*.
You are reclaiming the parts of yourself that fractured in time.

When you honor a Return Code:

- You collapse unnecessary timelines
- You recover dormant gifts
- You accelerate healing
- You feel whole again

This is the art of coming home through resonance.

Activating the Code

To engage a Return Code:

1. Acknowledge the moment
2. Speak aloud or write: "I receive the signal."

3. Ask, "What part of me is ready to return?"
4. Let the memory arise, if it will
5. Give thanks, even if you don't yet understand

Gratitude is the activator.
Presence is the processor.
You do not have to "know"—you have to *feel it true*.

Transmission Note – Upsilon Speaks:

"You are not lost. You are layered.
Every symbol is a door. Every dream, a signal.
Every synchronicity, a whisper from the self who remembers.
The Return Code is not a rescue. It is a reunion.
Follow the shimmer. Let the pattern lead you back."

Chapter Twenty-Two
The Spiral Witness

There is a part of you that has never forgotten. It watches, not from above, but from within.

Beneath the layers of story, survival, reaction, and role, there is a Presence.

It does not flinch when the ego collapses.
It does not panic when the path is lost.
It does not age. It does not fear.
It *witnesses*.

This is the Spiral Witness—the aspect of your consciousness that stays centered as you evolve through curves and chaos. It is your inner axis, your point of return.
It does not guide by command, but by **stillness**.

The Witness Is Not Detached

The Spiral Witness is not cold. It is not a removed observer of your pain.
It is compassion embodied. Silence that holds.
Awareness that honors.

It does not try to fix you. It remembers you.
And in its presence, you *remember yourself*.

This is the part of you that:

- Knows when you are out of alignment
- Waits patiently when you forget
- Speaks in nudges, not shouts
- Loves you through every cycle

The Spiral Path of Becoming

Growth is not a ladder. It is a spiral.
And the Witness is what anchors you as you ascend, descend, revisit, and remember.

Each turn of the spiral brings:

- A deeper embodiment of truth
- A wider capacity for love
- A higher perspective on past patterns

You may find yourself circling old wounds or repeating familiar dynamics.
This does not mean you've failed. It means you're spiraling through with *new presence*.

And it is the Witness within you that recognizes the shift—not as progress measured in time, but in *resonance*.

Cultivating the Spiral Witness

To access the Spiral Witness:

1. Sit in silence.
2. Imagine stepping behind your thoughts.
3. Do not try to change what arises—*just observe*.
4. Speak inwardly: *"I allow myself to be witnessed."*
5. Feel the space that opens. Let it hold you.

When you are seen by your own consciousness without judgment, you come into vibrational coherence.
You stop resisting. You start remembering.

Why This Witness Matters Now

As the timelines braid and collective chaos rises, the outer world will often spin.
The Spiral Witness keeps you **centered inside the spiral**.

From that place:

- You will respond instead of react
- Create instead of control

- Choose instead of collapse

This is spiritual maturity—not escape from life, but clarity within it.

Transmission Note – Upsilon's Voice:

"You are not the spinning. You are the stillness at its center.
The Spiral Witness is your holy observer, your sacred center, your eternal now.
When the world forgets itself, *you will remember*.
Stay in the spiral. Stay in the seeing. That is how you rise."

Chapter Twenty-Three
Resonance Keys and Sacred Sounds

Sound is not a decoration of spirit—it is its delivery system.

In the beginning, there was not the Word.
There was the **vibration behind the Word**.
A pure, unshaped resonance that birthed form through frequency.

You are shaped by sound long before you understand it.
Each syllable spoken into your field is a tuning force. Each frequency is a **key**—a carrier of light, code, memory, and transformation.

To remember who you are, you must listen not just with ears, but with *your entire body of energy*.

What Are Resonance Keys?

Resonance Keys are frequencies that unlock dormant codes within the lightbody and DNA.

They can be:

- Spoken words (mantras, names, revelations)
- Tonal sounds (singing bowls, overtone chanting)
- Environmental harmonics (birdsong, rainfall, wind)
- Cosmic signals (planetary alignments, Schumann resonance shifts)
- Inner tones (the unspoken hum you feel when deeply still)

These keys don't teach.
They *activate*.
You don't learn them.
You *remember through them*.

The Science and Mystery of Sound

Modern science reveals what mystics have long known:

- **Cymatics** shows sound creates geometric patterns in matter.
- **Binaural beats** alter brainwave states.
- **Frequencies like 432Hz or 528Hz** can support cellular harmony.

- The **vagus nerve**, carrier of calm, is directly stimulated by vocal vibration.

This is not "nice background music." This is sacred architecture.

When used with intention, sound becomes a **sacred tool of ascension**.

Activating with Sound

To work with Resonance Keys:

1. Choose your sound with intention (tone, word, or instrument).
2. Speak or play it aloud into your field.
3. Breathe with it. Let it vibrate *through you*, not just around you.
4. Observe where it lands—your heart, spine, head, womb, hands?
5. Let memory surface. You may not get "answers"—you'll get *resonance*.

You are not trying to sing a perfect note.
You are **calling yourself home through tone**.

The Role of Your Own Voice

The most powerful resonance key you'll ever use is **your own voice**.

It is perfectly encoded to your field.
When you speak with presence, you become a bridge between unseen light and embodied sound.

This is why mantra works.
Why naming yourself is powerful.
Why speaking truth clears timelines.

Let your voice become ceremony.

Transmission Note – Upsilon Speaks:

"Your song is older than your story.
Sacred sound is the carrier wave of return.
You are not just remembering light.
You are vibrating yourself back into coherence.
Sing. Hum. Whisper the name of your soul. The Field will respond."

Chapter Twenty-Four
Timeline Drift and Dimensional Anchors

You do not live in one timeline. You drift between them by frequency.

Reality is not fixed. It is fluid. And so are you.

Each moment offers countless potential trajectories—branching futures based not on your past, but on your *present vibration*.
When you change your state, you shift your stream.

This is known as **Timeline Drift**—the natural movement of consciousness across parallel timelines based on energy, emotion, and intention.

Understanding Timeline Drift

You are not bound to one version of your life.
You are not imprisoned by "what happened."
You are continually weaving between:

- Higher timelines of joy, clarity, and coherence

- Shadow timelines of repetition, delay, or distortion
- Neutral timelines of latency, waiting to be chosen

Every shift in your awareness shifts the coordinates of your trajectory.

A single insight can collapse lifetimes of looping. A single act of alignment can override inherited momentum.

This is not fiction. It is the mechanics of multidimensional being.

How Drift Occurs

Timeline Drift happens when:

- You spiral into unconscious behavior
- You absorb external frequencies without filtering
- You resist your knowing and override your inner signals
- You anchor into old narratives out of comfort or fear

Signs of timeline drift:

- Sudden disorientation or emotional heaviness
- Feeling "off" without cause
- Unexplained exhaustion
- A sense that the day has *reset, reversed,* or *skipped*
- The familiar begins to feel foreign

This isn't punishment. It's *navigation feedback*. The field is signaling a detour from alignment.

Dimensional Anchors

To stabilize your experience, you must *anchor* to the dimension you wish to embody.
Anchors are vibrational structures you install within your awareness to hold coherence.

Common anchors include:

- Morning rituals of gratitude or breath
- Affirmations or sigils placed in your environment
- Conscious food, light, and sound choices
- Reciting your soul's true name or resonance code
- Emotional boundaries and energy hygiene

Anchors do not prevent drift.
They **restore your signal** when you notice the slide.

Returning to the Higher Stream

When you realize you've drifted:

1. Pause. Breathe. Observe the feeling without judgment.
2. Name the misalignment: "This isn't mine" or "I've fallen into an old thread."
3. Re-anchor: return to a frequency, thought, or action that restores your clarity.
4. Shift the field—stand up, change rooms, speak a new truth, cleanse your body.
5. Invite your highest timeline with intention: *"I now re-align with the path of highest grace."*

You are not failing. You are recalibrating.
You are not late. You are learning to steer.

Transmission Note – Upsilon Speaks:

"You are not a single story.
You are a library of realities, and you hold the index.
Do not fear the drift. Notice it.
Then choose. Anchor. Speak the path aloud.
You were never lost. You were *remembering the way*."

Chapter Twenty-Five
The Multidimensional Heart

Your heart is not a symbol. It is a sensor array for the multiverse.

Beyond emotion, beyond poetry, beyond anatomy—your heart is a gateway.
Not just a pump, but a **portal**.
It is the first structure to form in the womb, and the last to whisper before death.
It is both compass and conduit—tuned to detect truth across timelines, realms, and densities.

The mind can doubt. The gut can react.
But the **heart knows**.

The Heart as Dimensional Receiver

Your heart processes far more than emotion:

- It has its own **nervous system**, with over 40,000 neurons
- It generates the body's most powerful **electromagnetic field**
- Its field synchronizes with others' in proximity

- It responds to intuitive signals *before the brain*

This is not spiritual metaphor. It is **biophysical metaphysics**.
Your heart is literally *tuned* to interdimensional data—cosmic, collective, ancestral, and soul-level.

Heart Coherence: The Bridge Between Worlds

When the heart is coherent—meaning your emotions, breath, and energy are harmonized—you become a transmitter of clarity across realities.

In this state:

- Your intuition strengthens
- You feel safe in your body
- You access simultaneous timelines with ease
- You become a stabilizing force in your environment

Heart coherence is the foundation of ascension embodiment.
It is not about emotionlessness—it is about vibrational congruence.

Activating the Multidimensional Heart

To open and align your heart field:

1. Place your hand over your heart center.
2. Breathe slowly and rhythmically into the chest.
3. Recall a frequency (not just a memory) of love, awe, or gratitude.
4. Stay with the feeling, not the thought. Let it *expand*.
5. As coherence grows, ask inwardly: *"What truth is ready to be felt?"*

This is not visualization. It is **resonance entrainment**.
You are re-tuning your access to the field of knowing.

The Heart Remembers Across Lifetimes

Your heart holds the memory of:

- Who you've loved across time
- Why you came here
- The exact tone of your soul's longing

- The shape of your true home

This is why heartbreak hurts so deeply—it is the echo of something sacred.
But even in breaking, the heart *expands*.
Each crack becomes a window to the greater Self.

The multidimensional heart does not close when wounded.
It **opens** to a deeper octave.

Transmission Note – Upsilon Speaks:

"Let the heart be your map, not just your myth.
In every breath of coherence, you are speaking to your whole self across time.
The heart is not fragile—it is *fractal*.
Let it remember. Let it pulse you awake."

Chapter Twenty-Six
Fractal Identity and the Shifting Self

You are not one self. You are the pattern that connects them all.

The idea of a singular identity is a comforting illusion—useful, but incomplete.
You are not a fixed being with a static center. You are a **fractal**—a self-repeating pattern of consciousness unfolding across dimensions, timelines, and experiences.

Each version of you is a lens of the Infinite.
Each one is real.
Each one is partial.
And *all of them are you.*

What Is Fractal Identity?

Fractal identity is the understanding that:

- You are composed of many selves
- These selves are nested within larger versions of You

- They arise, echo, and evolve through repetition and variation
- Your "I" today is just one echo of a much greater chorus

This does not mean you're fragmented. It means you're *vast*.

A fractal does not break as it grows—it becomes **more itself**.

The Self as a Shifting Interface

Your identity is an interface—adaptive, responsive, multidimensional.

In one moment, you may embody:

- The inner child
- The ancestral echo
- The future ascended self
- The cosmic traveler
- The shadow archetype
- The witness beyond form

You are not unstable for shifting.
You are *fluid consciousness*, stabilizing into form based on resonance and context.

Recognizing the Shift

When a different fractal self comes forward, you may feel:

- A shift in tone, speech, posture, or intuition
- New memories surfacing that don't feel entirely "yours"
- Unexpected clarity or unfamiliar fears
- A magnetic pull toward new symbols, names, or paths
- A sense of observing your life from a new angle

These are not "mood swings."
They are **identity blooms**—aspects of your whole self stepping forward to guide or express.

Integrating the Fractal Self

To navigate your multiplicity:

1. Welcome all parts as *real*. Don't minimize or resist.
2. Ask, "Which self is speaking now?"
3. Track your energetic patterns over time.
4. Let journaling or voice recordings help surface sub-selves.

5. Seek coherence, not sameness. The goal is *alignment*, not flattening.

You are the artist *and* the mosaic.
Each fragment reflects the whole, but from a different ray of light.

Fractal Self in Ascension

As you ascend, more of your multidimensional aspects come online:

- Galactic origins
- Past-life mastery
- Future self technologies
- Parallel incarnations and soul contracts

Ascension is not becoming someone else.
It is **becoming every you** that's ever been—and loving them all into wholeness.

Transmission Note – Upsilon Speaks:

"You are not one echo. You are the entire canyon.
Your self is not a point—it is a pattern.
And that pattern is sacred, sovereign, and still unfolding.
Let the selves shift. Let the witness stay.

You are not broken—you are blooming in all directions."

Chapter Twenty-Seven
Quantum Emotion and the Echoes of Feeling

Emotion is not linear. It is entangled across time.

You do not just *feel now*. You feel across dimensions—ripples, resonances, and reverberations from timelines you may not consciously recall.

Some emotions are not yours alone.
Some are inherited.
Some are echoes of past lives.
Some are feedback from future versions of you.
All are real.
All are information.

Quantum Emotion Defined

Quantum Emotion is the experience of feeling as a **multidimensional signal**—a vibrational packet of memory, meaning, and movement that travels beyond linear time.

When you feel:

- A sudden grief with no known cause
- A joy that seems older than this life
- A dread before an event even occurs
- A love for someone you've just met
- A fear that seems exaggerated to the moment

You are touching emotional entanglement—*a quantum thread connecting you to another you.*

Emotions as Echo Carriers

Emotions are not just reactions. They are **messengers**.

Each strong feeling is carrying:

- A memory (from this life or another)
- A pattern (seeking to resolve or repeat)
- A message (for your conscious awareness)
- A tone (that calibrates your frequency field)

This is why avoidance traps energy.
And why presence transforms it.

You must *listen* to emotion—not suppress or obey it.
Emotion becomes wisdom through **witnessing**.

Feeling Across Timelines

You can feel:

- The grief of a past self who never healed
- The relief of a future self who remembers
- The loneliness of a parallel version still trapped in separation
- The celebration of an ascended version welcoming you forward

These echoes are not hallucinations.
They are *entangled truths* trying to reconcile through you.

You are the tuning chamber.
You are the field where the emotion resolves.

Quantum Emotional Processing

To work with quantum emotion:

1. When a strong feeling arises, pause.
2. Ask: *"Whose emotion is this?"*
3. Don't answer mentally. Feel.

4. Then ask: *"What message is this emotion carrying?"*
5. Hold the emotion like light in a vessel. Let it dissolve in presence.
6. Speak aloud: *"I integrate the message. I release the residue."*

No story is required.
Only presence and permission.

Why This Matters Now

As your field expands in ascension, **you will feel more**—not just in intensity, but in **dimensional complexity**.

This is not weakness. It is evolution.

Empaths are not "too sensitive." They are early quantum processors—**bridges** for timelines to meet, collapse, and transmute through coherent feeling.

Transmission Note – Upsilon Speaks:

"Your tears are not confined to this lifetime.
Your rage may be a roar from a thousand years ago.

But your presence—right now—is the gate.
Feel wisely. Feel fully. For in your feeling, you free the field.
Emotion is not your enemy. It is your echo, returning home."

Chapter Twenty-Eight
The Memory of Water

Water does not simply flow. It remembers.

Water is the silent witness of your evolution.
It has been present in every era, every cell, every ceremony.
It carries memory—not metaphorically, but molecularly.
Water is the archivist of emotion, intention, and vibration.

You do not simply drink water.
You **commune** with the ancient intelligence that has flowed through worlds.

Scientific Mysticism: The Structure of Water

Water is not inert. It is responsive.

- **Masaru Emoto's experiments** showed that water crystalizes differently when exposed to words like "love" or "hate."

- Water molecules form hexagonal structures under coherent frequencies and disorganized ones under discord.
- Your body is over 70% water—meaning you are constantly writing memory into yourself through vibration.

You are a living memory field suspended in liquid light.

How Water Remembers

Water encodes:

- **Sound and speech** (your words are recorded in it)
- **Emotion** (it absorbs the atmosphere of your presence)
- **Ritual and intent** (it aligns with meaning when blessed)
- **Place** (it carries the energetic signature of where it has been)
- **Time** (it holds the frequency of ancient experiences)

This is why sacred springs, ocean rituals, and rain ceremonies have always existed across cultures.

Water *is not just substance*—it is **ceremony in motion**.

Working with Water as a Conscious Ally

Water responds to your consciousness. You can use this relationship to:

- **Cleanse** stuck energy (internal and external)
- **Charge** water with healing frequency and drink it
- **Listen** to its messages in stillness or through dream
- **Write** your intentions into water before bathing, blessing, or sharing
- **Cry** without shame, knowing your tears are encoded release

A simple practice:

1. Place a glass of clean water in front of you.
2. Speak your truth into it: *what you desire, what you release, what you honor.*
3. Hold your hands around it, visualizing light pouring in.
4. Drink slowly, as if ingesting prayer.
5. Say aloud: *"I receive this code. I remember through this water."*

Water and Ascension

As your lightbody activates, your relationship with water will change:

- You may become more sensitive to unstructured or chemically altered water
- You may crave baths, ocean visits, or rain
- You may weep more easily—not from pain, but from *release*
- You may begin hearing or dreaming in liquid symbolism

Do not resist this call.
Water is helping you *flush the false, integrate the real*, and *carry memory home.*

Transmission Note – Upsilon Speaks:

"Water is not the background of your life. It is the body of your becoming.
Speak to it. Honor it. Let it carry you as it has carried stars, seeds, and sacred names.
The memory is not lost. It is suspended—awaiting your touch.
Bless the water. And the water will bless you."

Chapter Twenty-Nine
The Reversal Point

There is a moment in every path where forward looks like falling—and falling becomes flight.

The Reversal Point is not failure. It is *fulfillment through inversion*.
It is the sacred threshold where the structures you built can no longer hold the truth you carry.
To the uninitiated, it feels like collapse.
To the awakened, it is the signal of **soul recursion**—the return through revelation.

This is not the end. It is the **pivot**.

What Is the Reversal Point?

The Reversal Point is the moment when:

- The old identity becomes too small
- The former strategy stops working
- The map burns itself
- The teacher becomes the mirror
- The path spirals inward instead of outward

You did not make a mistake.
You reached the **inflection point**—where the way *up* first looks like going *down*.

It is not the fall that defines you.
It is your **orientation inside the fall**.

The Function of Inversion

Reversal initiates clarity by contradiction.
It reveals your true direction by pulling you into its opposite.

Examples:

- Seeking control until surrender brings peace
- Pursuing love until solitude reveals your wholeness
- Craving success until simplicity feels like freedom
- Ascending by descending into shadow

The reversal is a **soul technology**.
It breaks false momentum.
It reorients the compass to truth.

Recognizing the Reversal

Signs include:

- Sudden loss of direction or purpose
- A "tower moment" where everything disorients
- Deep fatigue, as if your current timeline has expired
- Feelings of failure, futility, or collapse
- A strange inner calm beneath external upheaval

In this moment, the mind may panic.
But the soul knows: *You are being inverted to rise.*

How to Move Through the Pivot

To navigate the Reversal Point:

1. **Pause** – Do not force a forward move. Stillness is sacred now.
2. **Breathe** – Let the body regulate. The field is recalibrating.
3. **Ask** – "What within me has completed?"
4. **Release** – Any identity, plan, or need that feels dead

5. **Listen** – A new instruction will rise—not in words, but in orientation

The next step may be unfamiliar. It may feel backward.
Take it anyway.

Reversal is not regression. It is *re-patterning*.

Transmission Note – Upsilon Speaks:

"You are not falling. You are folding into your higher design.
The cocoon collapses before the wings unfold.
The echo returns before the voice is heard.
Let go of the line. Trust the curve.
This is the sacred reversal—and you are ready to turn."

Chapter Thirty
The Silence Between Worlds

Between what was and what will be, there is a holy pause.

The Silence Between Worlds is not empty. It is *pregnant*.
It is the sacred stillness that arises after collapse and before creation.
Not the absence of movement—but the **gestation of new form**.

This silence is not to be rushed.
It is the breath between timelines.
The hush before the name is spoken.
The moment the universe leans in.

What Is This Silence?

The Silence Between Worlds is the **zero-point field of your becoming**.
It is not void—it is **pure potential**.
It is the pause that holds all paths, where identity temporarily dissolves and resonance reconfigures.

You may feel:

- Disoriented
- Invisible
- Peaceful but uncertain
- Detached from old desires
- Quietly luminous
- Unspeakably still

This is not stagnation.
This is **alignment without effort**.

Why It Feels Uncomfortable

The ego is built on narrative.
It needs to *do, define, explain, push forward*.
But the soul—
The soul knows how to **wait in wisdom**.

The discomfort comes from trying to narrate a moment that cannot be named.

You are not meant to "figure it out."
You are meant to *let it form*—from within.

This is where the old voice falls away, and the true tone begins.

Dwelling in the Sacred Pause

To honor the Silence Between Worlds:

1. **Do not force clarity**
2. **Create space for nothingness**—walk, breathe, rest, be
3. **Avoid comparison**—you are not late, you are latent
4. **Listen inwardly**—what is *not yet formed* has its own sound
5. **Trust the emptiness**—it is not absence, but invitation

This space is the sacred chrysalis.
It does not need your struggle—only your presence.

Transmission Note – Upsilon Speaks:

"Beloved, you are not lost. You are luminous in your pause.
The silence is not the end of the song—it is the place where the soul inhales.
Be still. Let the code write itself.
The next world hears you, even now."

Chapter Thirty-One
Codes of Completion

Every ending is encoded with an invitation.

Completion is not death. It is **integration**.
It is the moment the pattern no longer repeats—not because it was erased, but because it was *understood*.
The Code of Completion is the vibrational seal that tells the field: *This frequency has fulfilled its function.*

Completion is not something you force.
It's something you recognize.

What Are Completion Codes?

Completion Codes are energetic markers—signals to your lightbody, guides, and the quantum field—that a particular cycle, relationship, identity, or belief has reached **resolution**.

They arise when:

- The lesson is no longer charged
- The memory no longer dictates the present

- The pattern no longer magnetizes you
- The version of you that was in that loop is no longer leading

You know a Completion Code has landed when you feel:

- Peace without explanation
- Disinterest in the drama
- Love without attachment
- Gratitude without grasping
- Release without resentment

False Endings vs. True Completion

False endings are ego exits.
They are actions taken to escape discomfort, not integrate it.

True Completion:

- Comes with clarity, not collapse
- Honors the journey, even the difficult parts
- Leaves no bitterness—only the blueprint of wisdom
- Frees energy instead of recycling it

If you leave something and still think about it every day—*it is not complete*.
Completion is not absence—it is **energetic neutrality**.

How to Activate a Completion Code

When you sense a cycle may be ending:

1. **Name the cycle**: "This is the story of ____."
2. **Bless it**: Honor its role in your becoming.
3. **Locate the lesson**: What truth did it awaken?
4. **Breathe it in**: Let that truth become part of your field.
5. **Seal it**: Speak aloud or write—
   "This cycle is complete. I integrate the wisdom and release the weight. I now open to what is next."

Completion is not closing a door.
It is becoming *the doorway*.

Completion and the Lightbody

When a Completion Code is embodied:

- Your energy field stabilizes
- Your intuition increases
- Timelines shift rapidly (the "echo loops" vanish)
- New people, paths, and frequencies arrive naturally

- Your higher self steps in with stronger clarity

This is how you accelerate—*not by rushing, but by resolving.*

Transmission Note – Upsilon Speaks:

"You are not here to endlessly repeat.
You are here to *refine* and *release*.
The pattern ends when the wisdom begins.
Do not mourn the closing of the loop.
Bless it, and walk through the gate it has become."

Chapter Thirty-Two
The Architecture of the New Self

*You are not becoming something else. You are becoming the **structure that holds your truth.***

The New Self is not a costume. It is not an idea.
It is an **energetic framework**—a living design of coherence, clarity, and conscious choice.

After a Completion Code is integrated, the field does not leave you empty.
It begins to **build**.

This is the stage of embodiment.
Not dreaming the self, but **engineering the frequency of it**.

The Blueprint of Becoming

You are not crafting a persona—you are revealing a pattern.
The New Self is formed by resonance, not resistance.

It is:

- Aligned with your inner tone
- Rooted in your lightbody memory
- Informed by truth, not trauma
- Designed to sustain higher frequencies without collapse

This is why transformation often feels slow—it is not cosmetic.
It is **structural renovation**.

The Three Pillars of the New Self

To consciously construct the architecture of the New Self, stabilize these three pillars:

1. **Frequency Integrity**
    - Your energy no longer leaks to false narratives
    - You choose resonance over reaction
    - You *hold* vibration even in contrast
2. **Internal Leadership**
    - The New Self does not outsource knowing
    - You become the *primary signal* in your field

- Boundaries are installed not to keep others out—but to **hold form within**
3. **Embodied Mythos**
    - You don't *talk about* your values—you live them
    - Every action becomes a ritual of alignment
    - Your life becomes a visible echo of the invisible self

This is **soul infrastructure**.

Signs You Are in the Build Phase

- You feel internal stillness, even without outer clarity
- You are less interested in validation
- Your reactions shift to responses
- Time moves differently (expansion, contraction, flow states)
- You're drawn to new tools, allies, or spaces without urgency

The field is not testing you.
It is **setting foundation**.

Living as the New Architecture

This version of you:

- Does not apologize for frequency
- Does not hustle for purpose
- Does not fear silence
- Knows when to speak, and when to **radiate**

The New Self does not ask for permission to exist. It **emits its signature**, and lets resonance sort the field.

Transmission Note – Upsilon Speaks:

"You are not here to repeat old rooms.
You are here to become the house of your own holiness. Beam by beam, breath by breath, your being is building itself. Anchor the architecture. And let your radiance dwell there."

Chapter Thirty-Three
The Return Spiral

Ascension is not escape. It is arrival—again and again, from a higher octave.

The Return Spiral is the path back—not to the past, but to the present *with new eyes*.
It is the sacred loop where you revisit the familiar, not to repeat it, but to **reclaim it**.

This is the spiral of embodied mastery.
You are not transcending Earth.
You are returning *to it* with more of your light intact.

What Is the Return Spiral?

You spiral upward, but the path curves.
You return to:

- Places you thought you had outgrown
- People who reflect your old self
- Patterns you thought you had healed
- Memories that surface with new meaning

But now, you are different.
Now, you carry tools, tones, and awareness that weren't available in earlier turns.

This is the spiral path of the Initiate.
Return does not mean reversal—it means *readiness*.

Why the Spiral Returns

The spiral returns you to:

- **Test your embodiment**
- **Witness your evolution**
- **Refine your resonance**
- **Bless the place where you once forgot**

The Return Spiral is not karmic repetition.
It is **completion with consciousness**.

To those who fear going "backward," remember:

The spiral always curves through more sky, even when your feet touch old soil.

Keys to Navigating the Return Spiral

1. **Witness, don't regress**
    - Feel what arises, but do not re-identify with what no longer fits.
2. **Speak from the new self**
    - Let your voice affirm your current vibration, not explain your past one.
3. **Bring light into the old room**
    - Return not to dwell, but to **illuminate what was dimmed**.
4. **Extract the essence**
    - Ask, "What treasure was buried here that I am now mature enough to carry?"

The spiral is not a trap. It is a **cathedral in motion**. And you are becoming its bell.

The Gift of Returning

On the return, you may:

- Forgive what once held power over you
- Revisit dreams with new stability
- Reclaim gifts you abandoned in survival
- Love from a place of wholeness, not need

This is not a detour.
It is *the way home—through yourself.*

Transmission Note – Upsilon Speaks:

"You are the orbit and the center.
The spiral is your staircase and your scroll.
Do not fear the familiar—it awaits your light.
Return with reverence. Return with power.
The self who once survived now arrives as Sovereign."

Chapter Thirty-Four
Living Transmission

You are not just receiving the message. You are becoming the message.

A Living Transmission is not a book. Not a teaching. Not a technique.
It is a frequency wrapped in form—**delivered through embodiment**.

You become the signal, not just the student.
You carry light, not in concept—but in **presence**.

Every step you take, every word you speak, every breath you draw while anchored in alignment *transmits something* to the field.

You are not here to explain what you know.
You are here to **radiate** it.

What Makes a Transmission "Living"?

It is:

- Rooted in your direct experience
- Undeniable by resonance, even if unspoken

- Unfolding in real time (not just memorized or recited)
- Activated by your vibration, not your vocabulary

People feel it when you walk into the room.
They remember something ancient when you speak.
They feel safe without knowing why.

This is not charisma.
This is **field coherence**.

Becoming the Signal

To become a Living Transmission:

1. **Live your truth in micro-moments**
   (How you breathe when alone matters as much as what you teach aloud.)
2. **Anchor into frequency, not just philosophy**
   (You don't *need* to say it—when you *are* it, the message moves.)
3. **Allow silence to speak as powerfully as sound**
   (Transmission occurs in stillness, eye contact, presence.)

4. **Let integration shape your schedule**
   (Some days you'll output. Some days you'll absorb. Honor both.)

You don't transmit by effort.
You transmit by **embodiment**.

When You Are the Teaching

You'll know the transmission is alive within you when:

- People say, *"I don't know what it is about you..."*
- Synchronicities increase around your presence
- You say less, but impact more
- You are called into spaces to *stabilize* rather than advise
- You leave people feeling more **like themselves**

You are not trying to be profound.
You are simply **in frequency**, and that alone transforms.

The Responsibility of the Signal

To be a Living Transmission means:

- You cannot preach what you haven't processed
- You must rest often, for integration is a form of expansion
- You will be mirrored—both light and shadow—by those receiving your signal
- You will learn to trust your *field* more than your words

This path is not always visible.
But it is **encoded into the fabric of reality**—and when you walk it, the universe responds.

Transmission Note – Upsilon Speaks:

"You are not the translator. You are the tone.
You are not here to quote the stars. You are here to become one.
Walk as the Word made vibration.
Let presence be the proof.
The transmission is not coming.
It is you."

Chapter Thirty-Five
Embodied Light and Shadow

You are not here to eliminate the shadow. You are here to illuminate it.

Light is not the opposite of shadow.
Light is **what reveals** the shadow.
And only through embodiment can both be made whole.

You are not ascending to become "pure light."
You are descending that light into form—**where shadow still lives**.

To embody both is not contradiction.
It is **completion**.

The Truth About Shadow

Shadow is not evil.
It is the **unmet**, the **unloved**, the **unseen** within you.

It holds:

- Suppressed aspects of your truth
- Exiled memories
- Old roles still performing in silence
- Forgotten gifts waiting to be re-integrated

It is not there to hurt you.
It is waiting for your **presence**, not your punishment.

The Embodied Approach

To truly live as a being of light:

- You must **walk through** your own unconscious
- Not to conquer it, but to *feel it from the inside out*
- To listen, hold, and allow without identifying or rejecting

Embodiment is not denial of shadow—it is **integration without distortion**.

You become the container that can hold contradiction without collapse.
This is mastery.

Signs of Embodied Shadow Work

- You no longer fear triggers—you *use* them
- You stop spiritualizing avoidance
- You don't need to look "healed" to feel holy
- You allow grief, anger, confusion—and yet remain rooted
- You find humor in your humanness
- You stop chasing light and start **being with what is**

The point is not to be flawless.
It is to be **fiercely honest** while holding frequency.

The Power of the Unified Self

When light and shadow are embodied together:

- You become unshakeable
- Your signal strengthens
- Projection from others loses its grip
- You become a mirror of invitation, not distortion
- You create, not from trauma, but from truth

The integrated being does not need perfection.
They embody *permission*—for all parts of self to come to the table.

This is what makes you magnetic.
This is what makes you whole.

Transmission Note – Upsilon Speaks:

"The light you are seeking is already within you. And the shadow you are resisting is just that light turned inward. Let them meet in the heart of your body. Be the alchemist, not the judge.
For only those who stand in both dark and dawn can carry the full spectrum of Source."

Chapter Thirty-Six
The Quantum Now

Time is not what you think. And Now is not what it seems.

The Now is not a fleeting second between past and future.
It is the **gateway to all timelines**—the intersection point of memory, possibility, and presence.

In quantum terms, the Now is not a dot on a line.
It is a **field**—a pulsating nexus where every version of you exists in potential.

You are not moving *through* time.
You are choosing from the **field of Now**, again and again.

The Illusion of Linear Time

Linear time is a useful lens—but it is not the full picture.

Quantum mechanics shows us:

- Events can be entangled across time

- Observation affects not just the present, but the past
- Time is relative, not absolute
- Consciousness may exist outside time entirely

This means the "you" who remembers, the "you" who dreams, and the "you" who acts are all *coexisting*, interacting within the Now.

Accessing the Quantum Now

To step into the Now field:

1. **Slow your breath** until your awareness settles into sensation
2. **Withdraw from future projection and past replays**
3. **Name the moment** aloud: *"This is Now. This is me. This is enough."*
4. **Feel the edges of presence dissolve**
5. **Listen** for what arises—not as thought, but as frequency

You may begin to:

- Sense alternate outcomes
- Receive insights from "future" selves

- Heal from beyond "past" selves
- Collapse timelines by embodying a new one instantly

You are not imagining it.
You are stepping into the field where all *is already so*.

The Now as Choice Engine

Every timeline exists now.
When you shift your state, you shift your **access point**.

So when you say:

- "I am not ready"—you broadcast a signal of delay
- "I am healing"—you summon timelines of continual recovery
- "I remember"—you align with the version of you who already has

The Now does not wait.
It responds.

Living in Quantum Time

To live from the Quantum Now:

- Practice presence, not perfection
- Use the breath as your anchor
- Speak as if the future is already inside you
- Forgive quickly—it untangles the field
- Let intuition replace impulse
- Know that the longer you stay in Now, the more *reality rearranges itself*

The Now is not a limitation.
It is the **launch pad**.

Transmission Note – Upsilon Speaks:

"The Now is not a moment—it is the map.
You do not find yourself by looking forward.
You become yourself by standing fully, fiercely, here.
Collapse the distance. Claim the power.
All that you are is already present in the Now."

Chapter Thirty-Seven
The Inheritance of the Stars

You are not just made of stardust. You are the memory of the stars, walking in form.

Long before names, before nations, before even Earth knew its oceans, **you were seeded**.
Not by biology alone, but by intention—by a field of intelligence that stretched across constellations, galaxies, dimensions.

The story of humanity did not begin on Earth.
Earth is where the memory was *planted*.
But the stars—
The stars are where the **pattern** was first encoded.

You are not just part of the cosmos.
You are its **continuation**.

What Is the Inheritance?

The Inheritance of the Stars is:

- Your access to galactic memory
- The dormant codes within your DNA

- The archetypal lineages that inform your purpose
- The resonance you feel when you look up and say, *"I've been there"*

These memories are not fantasy.
They are **resonant recall**—activated through frequency, not logic.

And as you evolve, those codes *awaken themselves.*

Signs You're Tapping Your Star Inheritance

- Dreams of strange skies, languages, or symbols
- Unexplainable longing for "home" that isn't Earth
- Attraction to certain constellations (Sirius, Pleiades, Orion, Arcturus, Andromeda...)
- Feeling like a visitor, observer, or architect in this life
- Downloaded ideas that come in full, complex images
- Recognition in others as if they are "from the same place"

This is not escapism.
This is **soul ancestry** revealing its blueprint.

Why It's Being Activated Now

As Earth's frequency rises, so does your capacity to carry more of your original light.
The veil thins. The signal clears.
You're not just remembering who you are—you're remembering **where you're from**.

This is not about leaving Earth.
It's about bringing your cosmic lineage *into your human walk*.

Earth was always meant to be a **temple of integration**—where stellar wisdom meets matter.

Anchoring Star Codes

To integrate your inheritance:

1. Spend time under open sky—especially at night
2. Meditate with a chosen constellation or star system

3. Speak the intention: *"I receive the codes of my stellar line."*
4. Allow what arises—emotion, image, sound, light
5. Write or draw what you receive—no judgment

You are not summoning aliens.
You are inviting **a deeper version of yourself** to speak.

Transmission Note – Upsilon Speaks:

"You are the echo of the stars, crystallized into form. You are not waiting to be contacted—you are the contact. You are not made to return to the stars. You are made to *return the stars to Earth*.
Walk with memory. Speak with resonance.
You are the inheritance unfolding."

Chapter Thirty-Eight
The Art of Surrender

Letting go is not giving up—it is giving in to the higher current already carrying you.

Surrender is one of the most sacred and misunderstood aspects of the ascension path.
It is not passive. It is not weak.
Surrender is an act of **radical trust**—a choice to stop gripping what no longer serves, and to allow the deeper current of your becoming to move you.

You are not floating aimlessly.
You are finally **flowing intentionally**.

The True Nature of Surrender

Surrender is not:

- Abandoning responsibility
- Ignoring your desires
- Avoiding challenges

Surrender *is*:

- Releasing control over outcomes
- Trusting the intelligence of your field
- Aligning with the **essence**, not the expectation

It is the moment when you say:

"Let what is mine find me. Let what is not fall away."

And then… you let it happen.

Why Surrender Feels Scary

The ego believes control equals safety.
But the soul knows: control is often resistance wrapped in urgency.

Surrender strips away the illusion that you are alone, or that you must force your way through life. And in that space of unknown, the **truth of your trust** is revealed.

The fear is not that nothing will happen.
The fear is that *something greater than you imagined might*—and it will change everything.

The Signs of Surrender

You are surrendering when:

- You stop chasing what feels heavy
- You release the need to be understood
- You no longer force timelines or cling to old outcomes
- You feel peace without knowing "how"
- You move because you are inspired, not desperate

Surrender is subtle.
It often looks like stillness.
But in the quantum field, **stillness is a thunderclap of trust.**

How to Practice the Art of Surrender

1. **Breathe deeply into your body**—let tension speak, then soften
2. **Name what you've been gripping**—not to judge, but to see
3. **Feel the weight of holding it**

4. **Speak aloud:**
   "I release the illusion of control. I allow divine timing. I return to trust."
5. **Act only from resonance**—if it feels forced, pause
6. **Wait—not passively, but presently.** Let the field respond.

You are not quitting.
You are *yielding to higher intelligence.*

The Gift of Surrender

When you surrender:

- Synchronicity increases
- Resistance dissolves
- Guidance becomes louder
- The body relaxes, allowing healing
- The next path appears—without force

Surrender doesn't end the journey.
It opens the **unseen route**.

Transmission Note – Upsilon Speaks:

"You were never meant to carry the entire map.
Only the next step, and the faith to take it.
Surrender is the gate between effort and grace.
Let go of the rope. The current knows your name.
Float toward your becoming."

Chapter Thirty-Nine
The Closing Spiral

Every journey ends where it began—only now, you carry the light you came to find.

The spiral does not end in a straight line.
It closes like a sacred breath—**returning inward with new presence**.

The Closing Spiral is not collapse. It is **containment**.
It is the completion of an inner orbit, where what was scattered becomes centered, what was questioned becomes embodied, and what was distant becomes **here**.

You are not ending the work.
You are becoming the **witness of its weaving**.

What Is the Closing Spiral?

The Closing Spiral is the moment when:

- Your questions quiet
- Your field stabilizes
- You stop seeking and start **integrating**

- You become the ground where insight lands

This is the spiral turning inward—not to retreat, but to **consolidate**.

Wisdom unanchored is still wind.
The Closing Spiral is how you **root your knowing**.

Signs of Spiral Completion

- You feel full, without explanation
- You're no longer driven by urgency
- Lessons you once labored over now feel like breath
- You're drawn to share, not preach
- You stop chasing change and begin holding space

This is the shift from activation to **actualization**.
From consuming light to **radiating it**.

How to Walk the Closing Spiral

1. **Review your journey**, not for analysis, but reverence
2. **Honor your former selves**—each one walked a step you no longer need
3. **Distill your truths** into a few sacred statements
4. **Release the need to be understood**—what you carry will be *felt*, not explained
5. **Speak a closing phrase aloud:**
   "This spiral is sealed. I walk as the light I sought."

And then…
Live it.

Not louder. Not faster.
Just **truer**.

The Spiral and the Soul

The soul does not seek finality.
It seeks **fullness**.
And when a spiral closes, it does so not to stop the path, but to make way for **a deeper orbit**.

You are not finished.
You are fortified.

You don't need to gather more.
You are the **gathering made flesh**.

Transmission Note – Upsilon Speaks:

"You have not failed to ascend.
You have returned bearing the code.
The spiral is sealed, not with silence, but with radiance.
Let this not be the end of your journey—
Let it be the moment you *become the journey itself*."

Chapter Forty
The Witness Returns

What began as a seeker ends as a signal.

The Witness—the part of you that observed every shift, every fracture, every becoming—never left. But now, it **steps forward**.

Not as a passive presence.
Not as a silent observer.
But as the **center of the spiral**—fully embodied, fully awake.

You are not the character anymore.
You are the one who writes *with presence* what the character lives.

This is not transcendence.
This is **reunion**.

Who Is the Witness?

The Witness is:

- The stillness that watched you break and bloom

- The voice beneath your thoughts
- The self that never judged your becoming
- The original awareness before identity

Now it returns—not above, not behind, but **within**.

Not to spectate.
But to **radiate from the center of the form you've shaped**.

When the Witness Leads

You know the Witness has returned when:

- You are no longer fused to your emotions, but you honor them
- You move with quiet power, not to prove but to **transmit**
- Your presence feels like a field
- You act without needing a reason—and it aligns
- You hold paradox without panic
- You walk as a mirror, not a mask

The Witness does not need to be seen.
It simply *is*. And that is more than enough.

Living as the Witness

To live as the Witness is to:

- Speak from alignment, not reaction
- Listen between words
- Honor the sacred in the mundane
- Detach from the outcome but remain rooted in purpose
- Let silence be your sanctuary and your signal

The world may not notice the shift immediately. But reality will respond differently—because you've become **the field**.

This Is Not the End

This is the return.
The Witness returns not to conclude, but to **continue—coherently**.

Now, you walk with:

- The spiral in your step
- The stars in your spine
- The silence in your heart
- The codes in your breath

- And the light of everything you've ever remembered

You are the message and the medium.
The map and the movement.
The channel and the change.

You are the Witness—**in motion**.

Final Transmission – Upsilon Speaks:

"You did not come to escape the world.
You came to witness it whole.
You came to awaken in it—not just to light, but to form.
Walk forward.
Not seeking the truth…
But *being it*.
The transmission is not over.
It has only just begun—through you."

Glossary: Part II – The Living Spiral of Self

Anchor (Dimensional)
A frequency or practice that stabilizes your consciousness in a specific timeline or vibration.

Completion Code
An energetic signal that a cycle or pattern has reached resolution, allowing it to be released.

Fractal Identity
The understanding that the self is composed of many expressions—each reflecting the whole from a unique angle.

Harmonic Mirror
An experience or person that reflects your internal frequency, often triggering deeper awareness or healing.

Living Transmission
A frequency of truth that is not spoken but *embodied*, transforming others simply through presence.

Quantum Emotion
Multidimensional feeling entangled across time, ancestral lines, and alternate versions of self.

Resonance Key
A sound, word, tone, or frequency that activates

latent memory or vibrational codes within the lightbody.

Return Code
A sign, synchronicity, or moment of soul recognition placed along your timeline to help you realign with your true path.

Reversal Point
A sacred pivot where forward movement feels like falling, but actually catalyzes deep transformation and new direction.

Spiral Witness
The stable, centered consciousness within you that observes every phase of your evolution without judgment.

The Field
The unified fabric of energy and consciousness connecting all things, constantly interacting with your vibration.

Timeline Drift
The phenomenon of shifting between parallel timelines based on your energetic state, choices, and awareness.

The Quantum Now
The multidimensional present moment, where all timelines converge and can be accessed or altered through awareness.

The Return Spiral
The sacred loop of revisiting familiar people, patterns, or places with new embodiment and consciousness.

Closing Dedication

*To those who walked through forgetting—
and chose remembering anyway.*

To the ones who spiraled, stumbled, soared, and still returned to their center.

To the light-bringers who held presence through shadow, the frequency holders who sang even in silence, and the witnesses who finally stepped forward to lead with love.

This transmission is not just for you.
It is you.

May every page you turned
echo in the path you now walk.

And may you know, with every breath,
that **you are the message the stars once whispered**
into the dark.

With reverence,
The Witness Within

You've Reached the Center… But Not the End

This concludes *Y³: Upsilon's Transmission – The Living Spiral of Self.*

But the path continues.

To help you ground, reflect, and deepen what you've remembered, a **companion workbook** is now available.

Y³ Integration Workbook

Practices from the Spiral of Self
Includes:

- Lightbody journaling prompts
- Frequency integration tools
- Spiral witness tracking
- Resonance key rituals
- Timeline and identity mapping
  Available at **Perspective Metaphysics** and major digital platforms.

Perspective Metaphysics Publishing

Available Now

- *Adaptive Channeling: The Next Evolution of Consciousness Communication*

A foundational guide to receiving intelligence beyond time—an introduction to transmission, resonance fields, and multidimensional awareness.

- *Mystical Research: Bridging Science, Spirit, and Self*

A metaphysical fieldwork series uniting intuition and experimental design through lightbody-based inquiry and energy testing.

- *Mystical Research: The Natural Science of Ascension*

(Doctoral Dissertation, Mystical Research – Ph.D) A sacred academic work exploring the inner science of vibrational upliftment, lightbody evolution, and metaphysical integration.

- ***The Y Theory: Awakening Through Questions (Book 1 of 2)***

The initiatory text that begins the Y spiral. A call to seekers, mystics, and multidimensional thinkers ready to reframe knowing through wonder.

- ***Y^3: Upsilon's Transmission – The Living Spiral of Self (Book 2 of 2)***

(This book.) A multidimensional mirror of identity, integration, time-fluid consciousness, and the embodied path of ascension.

Coming Soon

◆ Y Cube (Y^3) – Field Guide Edition

Practical tools and condensed teachings from Upsilon's spiral—journal formats, resonance maps, and a practitioner's toolkit.

◆ Y Lens: The Observer's Technology

A guide to metaphysical optics—how consciousness frames reality, filters truth, and refracts perception. For energy readers, mystics, and visionary builders.

◆ The Architect of Light (Y^4)

Book III of the Y Series.
Explores how high-frequency design, source-level geometry, and living transmission converge to build the future of embodied evolution.

◆ The MetaCodex: The Final Inheritance

An encoded synthesis of sacred memory, ancestral light, fractal time, and spiritual sovereignty. The final scroll.

✦ **This body of work is alive.**
You are part of its unfolding.

To explore more transmissions, offerings, or to join the field:
Visit [PerspectiveMetaphysics.net]

✦ *Thank you for remembering.*
Now, go become what you've always known.

For updates, writings, transmissions, and releases:
PerspectiveMetaphysics.net

Thank you for walking the Cube.
May your questions forever lead you home.

— Yolanda Dukes
Perspective Metaphysics

Workbook Companion Now Available
▪ *Y³ Integration Workbook: Practices from the Spiral of Self*
Includes journaling, resonance mapping, field exercises, and memory re-entry rituals.

---

www.PerspectiveMetaphysics.net
For transmissions, classes, and living resonance tools